Goddess Has Your Back

How Wicca Can Help You
Raise Your Self-Esteem and
Make Your Life Magickal

Plus Rituals for the Whole Year

Moonwater SilverClaw

A QuickBreakthrough Publishing Edition

More copies are available from the publisher with the imprint QuickBreakthrough Publishing. For more information about this book contact: askawitchnow@gmail.com

This book was developed and written with care. Names and details were modified to respect privacy.

Disclaimer: The author and publisher acknowledge that each person's situation is unique, and that readers have full responsibility to seek consultations with health, financial, spiritual and legal professionals. The author and publisher make no representations or warranties of any kind, and the author and publisher shall not be liable for any special, consequential or exemplary damages resulting, in whole or in part, from the reader's use of, or reliance upon, this material.:

Other Books from Quick Breakthrough Publishing:

- The Hidden Children of the Goddess
- Beyond the Law of Attraction to Real Magick
- Be Heard and Be Trusted: How to Get What You Want
- Love Yourself to Financial Abundance and Spiritual Joy
- Darkest Secrets of Persuasion and Seduction Masters
- Darkest Secrets of Charisma
- Darkest Secrets of Negotiation Masters
- Darkest Secrets of the Film and Television Industry Every Actor Should Know
- Darkest Secrets of Making a Pitch to the Film and Television Industry
- Darkest Secrets of Film Directing

Praise for Moonwater SilverClaw:

"When I first met Moonwater I realized what a remarkable, compassionate person she is. Over time, I've seen how she works hard to kindly serve and encourage others through her spirituality and found myself moved by her dedication. She brings Wicca to life, enveloping you in the mystery and magick of the Craft. Her writing talent is amazing! Her kindness and even sense of fun is ever present throughout her writing. Moonwater expresses profound Wicca concepts through examples in her own life experience. Wicca actually saved her life. and empowered her to leave an abusive marriage, and this shows the power of this sacred path to positively change the course of our lives, too. Moonwater's stories personally inspire me, and I am confident that they will inspire you also."

– Rev. Patrick McCollum, internationally recognized spiritual leader working for human rights, social justice, and equality; the 2010 recipient of the Mahatma Gandhi Award for the Advancement of Pluralism.

"Moonwater's writing will give you a portrait of a woman who lives her faith, and whose life was saved by it. Because so many lives, my own included, were irrevocably changed by Wicca, were given new focus, new purpose, and perhaps most importantly, new personal power to realize one's dreams and ambitions. . . . It's a story about making your own happy endings, about rescuing yourself, and that, I believe, is what makes writing like this necessary."

– Jason Pitzl-Waters, blogger at WildHunt.org

"Moonwater's writing is like sharing a nice cup of coffee with a new friend, while you two are taking a walk in the woods. As a writer, Moonwater has found her Voice. And that voice has a LOT to teach all of us, from the young person who wants to know why she feels 'special ', to us seasoned practitioners of Wicca who can always benefit from a straight-forward review of the basics." – Angus McMahan, blogger, http://www.patheos.com/blogs/askangus/

Visit Moonwater SilverClaw's blog:
www.TheHiddenChildrenoftheGoddess.com

Moonwater SilverClaw

CONTENTS

DEDICATION AND ACKNOWLEDGEMENTS

This book is dedicated to the God and Goddess. Thanks to Sherry Lusk and Tom Marcoux for editing. Thanks to Judita Bacinskaite for rendering this book's front cover. Thanks to Kay Pannell for her guidance and friendship.

CHAPTER 1:
GODDESS HAS YOUR BACK

Would you like your Wiccan path to lift up your self-esteem?

Would you simply like to feel better?

This book helps you actually feel your connection with the Goddess on a daily basis—even moment to moment.

As I mentioned in my first two books, *The Hidden Children of the Goddess* and *Beyond the Law of Attraction to Real Magick*, Wicca saved my life and empowered me to leave an abusive marriage.

As a High Priestess, I have supported friends, family, and colleagues in times of need. My blog TheHiddenChildrenoftheGoddess.com gives me a weekly opportunity to support website visitors from over 138 countries.

This book gives *us* the space and time to really explore magickal practices, rituals, meditations and experiences that you'll find comforting and uplifting.

My journey upon this path began with meeting the Gods. The Gods showed me the true path to self love and acceptance. Where I saw nothingness and unworthiness, they showed me abundance and a unique specialness that I had.

Now I will let you in on a secret. *You have your own unique specialness that no one else has.* It is yours, and yours alone. This new path is yours to discover and walk. Just like my own path, your path is a beautiful discovery simply waiting for you. Prepare to step forward on this new, wondrous, and beautiful path.

Let's take the next step.

Secret of How to Do Magick

When I first started doing magick it was really hit or miss, most often *mess*. My spell work was just not as effective as I wanted it to be. What was I doing wrong?

If you have wondered the same thing, you have probably done similar mistakes. For example, I'd do a money spell, but I'd just get new problems!

The real problem was, like many people, I just wanted a big payday. What I didn't know was that this is really the wrong way to approach a lack of money.

Many, if not most, spells written today are focused on the external opportunities or even requesting gifts from the Gods. Focusing on just the external can create new problems.

What if I could tell you a **Secret of how to do magick** — in a way where you avoid ethics issues about money?

I have mentored a number of people about this *Secret.* Now I will share with you this Secret.

A phrase from the poem by Doreen Valiente entitled *The Charge of the Goddess* tells us how to do magick well. But many of us, like my younger self, just don't see it. The line I'm talking about is: "…if that which thou seekest thou findest not within thee, thou wilt never find it without thee."

This line invites us to look within as we approach our

magickal work.

Instead of focusing on how to get money from outside sources, focus within. How? Instead of asking for a handout from the universe, ask, **"How I can create more energy in myself to obtain my desire? How can I make myself open to more prosperity?"**

Let's get more specific. You have been laid off and need a new job pronto! Bills are pilling up fast.

Let's use a sigil for this purpose.

How to Make Your Own Personal Sigils

Imagine putting a magical intention into an object. Why would you do that? Wiccans do this because they want the object to hold power to help them realize a personal desire. For example, you may be job hunting and you want the power of the object—in this case, a sigil—to assist you to get the ideal job.

Making your own personal sigils is easy. Some time ago, author/artist Austin Osman Spare devised a method for creating sigils.

Since that time, a number of authors have discussed Austin Osman Spare's process of making sigils. One book I appreciate is Frater U. D.'s *Practical Sigil Magic: Creating Personal Symbols for Success.*

I have made a couple of my own additions to the process.

First, throughout history, witches made sigils out of virgin parchment. But that is quite expensive. Also if you're vegan and will not wear leather, you will want to use something else. Why? Parchment is typically made from sheep skin. So let's talk about a process devoid of parchment.

I use the heavier art paper, the kind that absorbs ink and which can be infused with different tinctures made with herbs. Watercolor paper is a nice choice, too.

What about inks? You could use one of the many magickal inks on the market. My favorite is Dragons Blood Ink. But magickal inks can be expensive. So you can make your own out of a high grade ink such as Winsor Newton ink or India ink. To make it a magickal ink just add some essential oil to it, like myrrh. Mix and consecrate.

You can even use Sharpie pens as author Peter Paddon suggests. Just make sure to designate specific pens for only magickal work. They'll be part of your set of magickal tools.

You can use different colors for different desires. Here is a short list of colors and meanings that I include in my book *The Hidden Children of the Goddess:*

- Red: sex, desire, vitality, strength
- Orange: charm, confidence, joy, persuasion
- Yellow: intellectual development, joy, intellectual strength
- Green: prosperity, abundance, fertility, money matters
- Blue: healing, protection, spiritual development
- Purple: the occult, power, magick
- Pink: love, friendship, compassion
- White: purity, innocence, peace, tranquility

Write out your desire on a scratch piece of paper; you can use a single word or a phrase. Some examples are:

- I want an ideal job for me at this time
- Happiness
- I need a new house
- Success

We'll now use the word "Success" as our example. Cross off all of the repeat letters in Success. You end up with S, U,

C, and E. (You want only one of each letter that appears in the word.) Next, scramble the letters, getting S, E, U, and C (for example).

Now comes the fun part: Combine the letters together in an image.

Success Sigil

Can you find the letters?

In this way you can make all sorts of sigils.

If you want to imbue it with a potion or tincture, this is the time to do it. You can either soak the paper in your tincture or brush it on. Either way you must let it dry. Overnight is best.

Now with this new image (of combined letters), inscribe it with your magical ink on your absorbent paper.

Now that you have the sigil, the next step is to breathe life into it with Pranic Breathing, also known as belly breathing. If you're familiar with yoga, you are probably familiar with Pranic Breathing techniques. Breathe in deeply; allow your stomach to inflate. Visualize pulling up energy from the earth. When you have built up enough energy in your lungs, blow it onto the sigil. This will charge it with your energy and further empower your intention.

Now place your sigil in a safe place and forget about it.

Forgetting about it is the toughest part of the whole process. This helps the magick work.

As you can see, making your own sigils is quite easy and fun. After some practice, you will be able to do them quickly and easily.

Remember the Gods are here to help. You can call on them for inner strength.

How to phrase a sentence for a sigil to get a job:

- All blocks I have put up, known and unknown, dissolve so that I am a good candidate and my future employer hires me.
- Help me express the inner strength, skills and energy so that I can acquire a job of my liking.

Here are phrases for those who have an interest in an entrepreneurial path:

- I find new ways to serve others successfully so that money comes to me naturally.
- All blocks I have put up, known and unknown, dissolve so that I can create abundance in my life.

Can you see how each sentence or phrase focuses on inner change, not the external "give me, give me"? With these phrases you are not looking for a handout. **You are creating the abundance by changing** *yourself.*

This can be applied to the rest of your magick as well. Another example is love spells. Focus your magick on *being more loving, or more open to love.* Never do love spells *upon* a particular person. Instead do a spell to attract love to you in whatever form is appropriate by creating yourself as more loving.

By focusing on inner change and developing our inner

strengths, we can achieve our desires.

Goddess Has Your Back in the Worst Times

When you're reading a book what are you looking for? I'm looking for the truth and some way to become stronger. I promise to provide both for you in this chapter.

So what have you heard about the burden of depression?

If you've experienced it, you know what an oppressive malady it is. If you have not experienced it, it's hard to convey the essence of the pain.

Ever since I was little, I've had feelings of hopelessness and unworthiness. Abuse in the form of beatings from my brother and neglect from my parents intensified my hopelessness.

I never knew when abuse would fall upon me. There was no rhyme or reason. Abusing a little girl is inexcusable. But what was worse, as that little girl, I felt a torrent of twisted thoughts. I believed the abuse happened because I deserved it.

I've heard that a number of people had a teacher that provided the support they didn't have at home. But I wasn't that lucky.

I did what I could to survive. I avoided people.

To me, depression was living in a deep, deep hole. A dark place where I was alone. I felt that I deserved this dark place. I had no hope, no love, no respect. I felt worthless. My chest hurt. Just cold putrid rotting meat inside me. The depression made it move and writhe like a carcass filled with maggots. There was more: tar, shards of broken glass, rusty nails.

Escape! That's all I wanted. At eight years old, I tried to hang myself.

The Gods intervened. The cord broke. Not just once, but every time I tried to commit suicide, the Gods saved me.

They poured their light into places I never thought any light could reach. My heart and soul. When that happened it was indescribable. It was beyond an epiphany. It was beyond life and death. It was so miraculous I can't describe the event. Only that it was life-changing in every way.

It changed my thinking, my speaking, my body. It changed my world. It changed me. I was not me anymore, and yet, I was. My memories were the same, my environment was the same, my story was the same.

I knew who I was and where I had come from. *But now it was all different.* How I experienced life was completely new.

I still have depression. However, I no longer identify myself as "a depressed person." I am a spirit who deals with depression symptoms. I take medication and I have a helpful therapist. Each day I have good moments. I reconnect with the Gods on a daily basis. Even as I write this, my altar gleams with a glowing candle.

The Gods gave me the gift of self-love. I want to show you the way to it. I can't walk this path for you, but I can show you my own path and walk side by side with you on yours.

How the Gods Changed My Perspective on Myself for the Better

One of the best exercises I learned for changing perspective was meditation. Through reflective meditation, the Gods helped me understand how skewed my perception of myself really was. This was a key turning point for me.

One thing you always hear about are affirmations. Numerous people meditate on affirmations, but for many of us these just don't work.

What is an affirmation? *The Merriam-Webster Dictionary* defines affirmation as "to validate, confirm, to state positively."

These affirmations didn't work for me either.

Why?

The problem with affirmations is a simple one:

With affirmations you are trying to lead yourself. The issue with that is you get in your own way. Like me, many people can't step aside and let the message in. They can instantly find examples or reasons that the affirmation is not true.

No matter how hard you may try to pound that new idea into your brain with the affirmation, your brain pounds back just as hard, if not harder.

Many people's inner self beliefs interfere with these positive statements. For an example, if I used the affirmation "I am thin," all my head says is "No, I'm not, just look in the mirror. It's not true."

So how did the Gods help me fix this problem?

With the following meditation that I learned from the Gods you can get around that problem with more ease than if you did not use this technique. Is this going to be easy? Probably not. Especially if you have a background like mine. Your subconscious will fight you all the way, as mine did. Still, it will be worth it.

A note on meditations: The sections in boldface are the words to be read aloud. The pauses within the text are places where you should stop speaking so that you can focus on visualizing and interacting with the astral environment. I recommend that you pre-record yourself saying the boldfaced words. Then, during the meditation, you can playback your recording. Just be sure to speak slowly and calmly and to include the long pauses in your recording.

For all meditations you should follow these simple

guidelines.
- Find a place where you will not be disturbed for the entire meditation.
- Take a sitting position where your spine is straight and your feet are flat on the floor.
- Dim light helps
- Take phone off the hook/turn off phone

Self Love Meditation

Close your eyes. Be aware of the light that is in the room through your closed eyelids.

Breathe in and out deeply . . . Relax.
Keep breathing.
Breathe out the stress of the day.
Breathe in relaxation and peace.

(Pause)

You are still aware of the light that is in the room.
Now the light begins to fade.
As it fades you feel total comfort. You feel safe and secure in the darkness.

(Short Pause)

Now, a new form of light blossoms. It surrounds and wraps you in its loving energy. This light is the light of the Gods.
It is a light of love and compassion. Take it in.
As you take this light and understanding in, you can now see with the Gods' eyes.
You can now see yourself as They see you—pure,

beautiful, whole. You are a masterpiece of their creation. You were made with love, and you are a manifestation of their love.

You are love.

This understanding fills you.

(Pause)

You know that even though you may leave the light at this time it is never truly gone.

With this new understanding you are now ready to return to the physical world.

It's a gentle transition as the light begins to fade around you once more.

Slowly at first. It gets darker and darker.

As it fades you feel total comfort. You feel safe and secure in the darkness.

(Short Pause)

Then a familiar light returns, the light in the room where you started.

It gradually gets brighter and brighter.

You are back in the room. You have brought the calm and peace and happy feelings back with you.

Now, gently open your eyes.

You can do this meditation as often as you need to. It may not take at first, but keep trying. Eventually the Gods' light will shine within you.

With this tool, I could now see what the Gods saw in me, not what other people said they saw. I wasn't this deformed disgusting person others had led me to believe. I was not overweight as a child, or stupid and ugly. I wasn't dishonest or rude. I was me, maybe not perfect, but I definitely was not those things they called me.

Learning to see myself with love and compassion was the first step on my road to self knowledge and growth. Understanding the truth helped me to change my perspective on myself. It was slow, but it did change and it's still changing. I still have to work on my self image. I am trying to undo an entire abusive childhood. I just need to keep reminding myself that it takes time.

With these tools I not only learned compassion for myself, but I learned compassion for others, too. I started to notice how poorly others were treating each other. I understood their pain.

Before this transformation started, when I was eight I tried my first suicide attempt. At this early age I understood how real the pain is. For some, the pain is just too much, and I understand.

Later in life I had a dear friend who committed suicide. He had depression, like me. I remember he had this great laugh and was so nice to everyone. But the dark side of depression is that people who have this horrible affliction are very good at pretending to be happy, pretending that there is nothing wrong. None of his friends or even his psychiatrist saw his death coming. Depressed people are very good at blending in much of the time, even if they are screaming and tearing at their flesh from the inside. This is one of the things that makes it so dangerous.

Unlike me, my friend completed his suicide. I miss him so much. Am I mad at him for doing it? No... I understand the monster that is depression. Mine is always with me. Telling me its lies, as it stares at me, with its cold burning eyes. But I am learning to deflect its gaze. Everyday I get better and better at it. It's a constant battle to not listen. And I fear it always will be.

But you know what helps me get through it? My Wiccan path and my relationship with the Gods.

The Gods gave me the gift of self-love. You can receive that gift as well.

I want to show you another way to augment the Self-Love Meditation above. Here is a chant you can recite to yourself when you're hurting:

<u>Healing Chant</u>
By the Sun and by the Moon,
Let the Gods' light be my boon.
Shining deep and shining far,
May I be healed by every star.
I saw it then, I see it now,
Darkness be gone right here, right now!

You can use this short chant whenever you are feeling low. For example, you can use this chant during meditation, by lighting a candle or as a prelude to the Self-Love Meditation from above.

As I said at the beginning of this chapter, Wicca saved my life. Now, I now try to help others through my books and blog: GoddessHasYourBack.com.

My utmost desire is to help others change their lives for the better as I have. If I can help one person not commit suicide because of how others have taught him or her to think, or if I can help one person not listen to the monster that is depression, then I will have accomplished something. To help that person conquer the pain and nightmare of his or her life would mean so much to me.

Now I invite you to take action to include the Self Love

Meditation and Healing Chant in your daily life.

Find the Benevolent Goddess

In the beginning I only knew one God—the God that my parents' church pushed upon me. This form of "God" was a cruel and unloving deity, someone who left me to sit in the misery and despair that was my life. The God I knew wasn't love and compassion. The God I knew was heartless; all He did was take and take.

When I was 10, the next-door neighbor's dog got ahold of our new kitten Moki and mauled her terribly. Moki was my only friend. She was my rock. I know this sounds sad, but I didn't have anything or anyone else at the time.

As my parents drove Moki to the emergency vet, I prayed and prayed as hard as I could. Little Moki gasped, her body twisting and contorting as she struggled to breathe. As she slowly suffocated in front of me, I still believed in this "God" that I had been taught to revere. But as I prayed and prayed for Him to spare my little friend; instead I helplessly watched her small body as it convulsed. Then... she was still. *He took her*, my only friend. He took her without mercy—just cruelty. She suffered greatly and her suffering was my suffering.

The following day, with tears streaming down my face, I pleaded with this "God." I said, "Why, why did You take her? The only thing good I had in my life?"

All I got was an uncompassionate cold shoulder from this "God" who was supposed to be this great all loving deity.

This "God's" indifference had me feeling worthless. I was unimportant and something to be ignored, just as my parents had taught me. I was alone and trapped.

Luckily, my later encounters with the Gods and

Goddesses of Wicca would turn out quite differently.

Finding Wicca

When I was growing up, my brother terrorized me. I never knew when he was going to beat me or torment me. My parents ignored me when I told them of the beatings. This was my childhood of terror and darkness. Full of torment, loneliness and sadness. Until one day I found a word, *Wicca*.

I don't remember how and where I heard this word. With curiosity in my heart, I went to the local bookstore and found *Wicca: A Guide for the Solitary Practitioner* by Scott Cunningham. My dyslexia made reading a slow, hard process. For example, sometimes, "p" would look like a "b" or "d." My depression symptoms would compound the problem by making it hard for me to focus on the words.

But I was so motivated to read this book, and I persisted.

This book opened me up to a beauty I had never before seen in the world. The book introduced me to the Lord (the God) and the Lady (the Goddess). It was as if a light pierced the darkness of my life and I was able to see the beauty around me for the first time. And this beauty started when I met the God and Goddess.

Wicca: A Guide for the Solitary Practitioner gave me the basics of meditation.

When I first sat down to meditate, my thoughts caused me trouble. I thought, "What's going to happen? *When* is it going to happen? Within five minutes, I gave up.

It felt like my mind was a squawking monkey. A squawking monkey on crack.

My mind functioned like a chattering monkey.

Buddhist refer to the "monkey mind."

Although I was tempted to quit my efforts at meditation,

the book's vision of the Gods and a wonderful world inspired me to keep going.

I wanted to see this beautiful world that the book described to me. I wanted to know it, feel it, and live it.

Probably, the toughest things holding me back were negative questions like: Was I worthy enough for this world and these Gods? Would I be accepted? Could I be loved? Would these Gods love me, take me into their hearts? Or would They reject me and cast me adrift back in my sea of unworthiness?

Fortunately, I could already feel something compelling me to go further. It pulled me and led me on, despite my doubts.

I couldn't see it at the time, but now I realize that the Gods were with me then, leading me to Them.

After about thirteen mediation sessions, something quite different occurred.

On a Fall afternoon, I sat on the deck at the back of the house my family owned in Redwood City, California.

My parents and brother were at the front the house, watching TV. I was alone. I was safe.

My eyes were closed. My breathing regular. My mind at last calm and clear. Then I sensed two beings near me.

The God appeared to me as a man of the forests and of animals. He smiled. The God was happy to see me.

And I felt something I had never felt before: joy.

I didn't understand it intellectually. My belief had been that I was worthless.

But the God welcomed me with pure love.

To my other side was the Goddess in the form of a beautiful woman with long hair reaching the small of her back. Next, I felt the energy issue from her hand as she took my right hand.

The God took my left hand.

No words were necessary. In an instant, I knew, felt it deep in my heart, that They loved me. They gave me the understanding that I was important and had a purpose.

Once They were sure that I understood, They began to fade away.

This moment was precious. I didn't want it end.

This was the moment I knew I was loved and important to Someone.

This was first time the Gods revealed themselves to me. All my questions were answered. I learned of Wicca and the Old Ways. This new world was exciting to me. There were so many possibilities and ideas that I could take root in. It was like seeing light for the first time, or hearing music when you had never heard such lovely sounds before.

Such was my epiphany.

Hand in Hand with the Gods

Since that meditation, the Gods continue to hold my hand and lead me through all my life challenges. Their love and compassion, keep my eyes open and focused on a completely different light.

Such light transcends boundaries. It has been *the most beautiful thing/presence/energy* I have ever experienced. When such light entered my life, it was like seeing my first brilliant dawn after a lifetime of blindness. Such brilliant colors plus a new warmth caressed me. All this beauty, color, and warmth was the Gods.

They taught me that I am loved. More than that: I *am* love.

The symphony of beauty revealed to me through the God's love drowned out the self doubt and self hate I had for myself. The Gods revealed the true me. My true essence shined in their brilliant light.

With the new knowledge They gave me, I was now aware of the truth. Before meeting the Gods, I had been buried in lies, perpetrated by the physical and mental abuse that I had lived through. Growing up, I was taught that I was worthless. The Gods showed me that this was nothing but lies.

With the Gods' love, I was shown a different path and a new light.

I will share the Gods' path of love with you.

The Big Difference When the Compassionate Goddess Supported Me through Grief

So I shared with you earlier about how I was a bereft child, terribly grieving over the death of my beloved kitten Moki. At that time, I only had a bitter, angry "God" idea slammed into me by my parents' church.

After my experience of meeting the God and Goddess, I had a epiphany that Someone really cared.

This was so helpful when my dear friend "Joe" committed suicide.

I gathered with my coven and the Goddess showed me that Joe was fine in the spiritual realm he had moved on to.

In fact, it was revealed to me that he had moved beyond what his church had taught him and that he had welcomed a peaceful alternative.

Now I invite you to continue on this journey with me through this book. We'll continue to explore how the Goddess (and God) can be reached and you can feel Their comforting.

CHAPTER 2
THE GODS HELP WITH SELF-ESTEEM AND SELF-WORTH

Imagine that you could see the Gods' view of you. As I implied in the first chapter, Their view holds you in compassion and love.

Being able to see the Gods' view when it came to myself was so important and it was the first step to growing my self-esteem and self-worth. How did I start my path? Simple, I learned one important and basic truth. I am of the Gods, and the Gods are of me. We are one. In Wicca we are not separate from the Gods. We, just like everything else, are part of the Gods.

This truth rocked my understanding of who I was then, who I am now and who everyone else is. Does this mean I have a "god" complex? No, or at least I certainly hope not. This doesn't mean I am better than others.

We are all equal in importance. We are all special, just like the strands of a spider's web or the pieces of a puzzle. We all have an important role to fulfill. Like the puzzle example, each piece is unique, but none is more important than any other. We are all unique and important, just like the pieces of a puzzle. The whole picture of the puzzle cannot be seen clearly if you do not have all the pieces.

Learning this truth shattered all the pre-conceptions of what I knew. This simple fact taught me that I couldn't be garbage, I wasn't worthless, and most important, I was connected to everything in the universe. I was a powerful, beautiful being. With this understanding I learned something invaluable. The only one who could lower me was myself. And by believing the people's lies about me, I put myself there.

People who feel insecure and fearful will always shove others beneath themselves to try and mask their own feelings of inadequacy. This not only hurts the people they step on but they are also hurting themselves by dishonoring the Gods. By lowering others, they disrespect the deity in others and in themselves.

How is this? All beings are part of the Gods. To hurt another being is to harm the Gods, and in doing so, you end up harming yourself. This is where The Law of Three comes into play.

The Law of Three is a simple law in principle. Basically it works like this: whatever action you send out into the universe comes back to you magnified. I have seen this law in action.

This worked in my personal life in many ways. For one, I kept throwing out all this negativity because of my self hate. With all that energy going out against myself I didn't get to experience anything positive in my life. This is where the Self Love Meditation (shared in Chapter 1) really helped me. With this meditation I was able to see the light of the Gods and in so doing see my own light.

The Gods helped me learn not to jump onto the bandwagon of self-hate that people shoved into my head. The Gods picked me up and dusted me off and showed me the way.

One of the things that helps Wiccans is to realize that better thinking leads to better magickal outcomes.

Thoughts We Think and the Magick They Create: the Good, the Bane, the Magickal

What have you been thinking about today? Have you paused for a moment and listened to the words you say to yourself?

We know that words have power. The words we say can create change of emotion, of how we are treated—and even change the world.

What kind of words do you say to yourself—as a habit?

Do your words include:

- Good effort. You're getting closer to what you want.
- That's okay. You've learned something. You'll do better next time.

Recently, a friend pointed out that some of my words were really unkind to me.

I then realized that I've had the habit of saying certain mean things to myself:

- I can't do this.
- I just made myself look like a f—ing idiot.
- I can't do anything right.

Wow—it hurts just to write that down!

Words are connected to our habitual thoughts. Many of

us don't really pay attention to what we tell ourselves on a daily basis.

As Wiccans, we need to pay attention to what we say because our thoughts and words hold power. If you repeat thoughts enough times, they become your reality. How is this true?

Let's look at one of the self-defeating thoughts I was telling myself: "I can't do this."

When I was younger, I wanted to be a writer. But my dyslexia kicked my butt. I told myself, "I keep getting it wrong so I must be a f—ing idiot. I can't do this."

I didn't come back to writing for 24 years.

So we see that your thoughts can actually cripple you. Your thoughts can kill your innate gift.

Don't let that happen. Become aware of your habitual thoughts.

Thoughts have their own magickal power. They can work for you or against you. They are a type of energy and they manifest your view of reality.

If you notice you are not feeling that great about yourself, ask these questions:

- What have I told myself lately?
- What have I been thinking about?
- Is it positive or negative?

Thoughts become beliefs if repeated often. This can be dangerous because these thoughts can manifest in our lives.

If you see negative things manifesting in your life, look at what you're telling yourself because the thoughts are being sent out and create what you see and how you see it.

We can replace negative thoughts with positive ones to create our own magickal transformation.

If you notice that you're putting yourself down, tell

yourself, "Stop! Reframe." One of my own coaches brought this "Stop! Reframe" technique to my attention. The idea is to break the pattern and then "reframe" the situation by telling yourself something positive. In essence, you're giving yourself a new way to perceive the situation.

This process works for many people.

Additionally, I came up with my own process. If I think something negative, I tell myself, "Stop! Goddess thought."

For example, sometimes I put too much hot sauce on the eggs I prepare for my sweetheart. (Yes, he likes hot sauce on eggs. Go figure.)

I'll say, "Damn it. That was dumb!"

Then I'll tell myself, "Stop! Goddess thought." I then step out of myself into the loving, compassionate energy of the Goddess. I then imagine what compassionate thing Goddess would tell me: "He'll be glad to get these eggs. You just saved him time and he was able to do more writing this morning. He always says something nice about receiving food that you make for him."

My point is that we Wiccans need to become our own best friend. Be the cheerleader of your own life. Remember our thoughts are always with us, just like the Gods. If you have trouble, ask the Gods for help. Look with Their eyes of compassion and love for you.

If you catch yourself making a cutting remark, say, "Stop! Goddess Thought." Then look upon yourself with the loving eyes of the Goddess. Imagine what She would say to you to lift you up and bless you.

Doing this, you can change your view and your life.

After we focus on thinking, it is now helpful to focus on breathing.

How a Wiccan Recovers Her Balance

As Wiccans, we make continuous efforts to stay in balance with nature. Right now much of the western U.S. is suffering through a heat wave.

Staying cool is important—not just as a convenience but staying cool can save your life! So we're turning up the AC (air conditioning) now.

As Wiccans, we endure other situations which throw us off balance and which require another form of "AC." Whether you're confronted with an argument with a family member or some driver cutting you off in traffic, you can see your temper get frayed.

In fact, I'm concerned about keeping cool and not getting irritable with others (even if they deserve it).

So how do you turn on your own AC during these heated times?

Breath control is a great way to calm down and control your words and actions.

Let's say you're stressed out and you're losing your cool. What can you do?

Breathe. Let's practice now. Take in a deep breath through your nose. In your mind count to three (a sacred number) slowly.

Hold your breath for two counts. And then breathe out for three counts.

Repeat this slowly through five repetitions.

How do you feel now? Many of us find ourselves calming down. That's really useful!

Remember breath control as your personal AC in a heated situation. Just as we refresh ourselves with breath control, it's valuable for us to regularly partake of ritual bathing. This is a marvelous way to feel cleansed and free of negative energy.

The Importance of Ritual Bathing

Imagine you could enhance your magick working with a simple process. How? Ritual bathing. It's important because it puts you into the right frame of mind before you perform ritual. Secondly, you physically clean your body of the dirt and grime of the day. Finally, ritual bathing cleanses you of the psychic garbage that clings to you as well.

You can choose any soap (a required part) that you prefer. Wiccans appreciate handmade soaps, especially if they already contain the herbs or essences they already use in magick work.

How do I make my bathing a ritual bath (or shower)?

Bless and consecrate your soap and shampoo. Set these aside for use *only* during your ritual baths.

How to make a sachet with cleansing herbs for a bath:

Use a stocking or cotton cloth, and place inside selected cleansing herbs. The total amount of all herbs will be one tablespoon.

If you use a cotton cloth, gather the corners and tie them with a string. Make sure the sachet is closed and secure. This keeps the herbs from clogging your drain.

Place your sachet in the bath water then sprinkle in some sea salt and let steep for 5 or so minutes. Then enjoy.

Making a cleansing shower brew:

If you will be showering, place your sachet in a large container of hot water to steep. Sprinkle sea salt and dissolve it into the mixture (the brew). When the water cools to a comfortable temperature, take it into your shower and wash with your consecrated soap, envisioning all the psychic garbage leaving you.

Then pour the contents of the brew over your head and rub it in. In this way, the contents help you complete your cleansing. The psychic residue flows away, down the drain.

Add a blessing

I also add a blessing at the end of my ritual bath. I've added some modifications to a popular blessing.

Wiccan Blessing

Starting at your forehead as you touch you third eye, say:

I bless myself by the Goddess,

(Touch your right breast)

By the air that is her sweet breath,

(Touch your left shoulder . . . [you are actually forming a pentagram with these movements].)

By the earth, that is her fertile body,

(Touch your right shoulder.)

By the waters that is her life giving womb,

(Touch your left breast.)

By the fire that is her bright spirit,

(Touch your third eye.)

May I be blessed, so mote it be.

Upon completing your ritual bathing, you're now ready to enter circle to honor the Gods respectfully. Not only will the Gods be happy but your fellow practitioners will be grateful, too. (Trust me.)

* * *

Since we've begun our discussion about performing rituals with ritual bathing, now is the time to identify important steps including invoking and banishing the

Element.

Invoking and Banishing the Elements

When we begin a ritual and call in the Elements, we are inviting them to protect us and help us with something we want in life.

For example, if I'm doing a ritual related to love, I may invoke Water because it focuses on emotions.

I may want to bring passion to some situation in my life, and I would then invoke Fire.

How do we invoke an Element? It involves moving your hand in the air to create a pentacle according to that element which is indicated in the diagram below.

Proper invoking is easy. All you need to know is where to start. Here is a good rule: To invoke, go towards the element you're invoking.

What this means is: you move your hand in the air (according to the diagram) in the direction of the desired Element.

At the end of the ritual, you will want to banish the Element. I've shared with a student that if you don't banish Water after you invoke it, you might end up with plumbing problems. If you don't banish Fire, you might have a fire start in your home. Don't let this happen! Be sure to banish the Element.

To banish the Element, move your hand in the direction away from that Element you wish to banish. You can see this in the diagram below (See next page).

Pentagram Chart

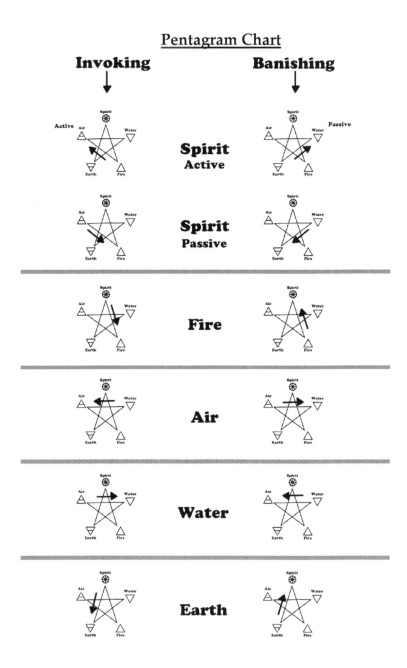

When do I use the elemental invoking and banishing pentacles? One of the most common ways to use these pentagrams is in casting and later taking down a circle. The other most common use is when you work with specific Elements.

Elements can be a powerful part of your spiritual practice. Handle with care.

And watch positive outcomes happen.

Since we have talked about invoking and banishing pentacles, now it would be helpful to talk about *grounding.*

Grounding and How It Helps You Get Rid of Extra Energy and Negative Energy

Once I started practicing the Craft, I came to realize that proper grounding is essential. It's just as important to ground as it is to practice at all.

When I was initiated into the Craft, I didn't "ground" properly after the ritual. Grounding is shunting extra energy out of your body. I failed to do the process.

Big mistake. I was up for 2-1/2 days. It was a double-edged sword: the energy was amazing, but I was bouncing off the walls. Now I was manic *and* tired. Headaches and body aches slammed me down.

My manic behavior annoyed the people near me. Worse yet—I put myself and others in harm's way when I drove my car. Tired and unfocused, I was of no use to anyone.

When I finally came down from the energy, I slept for three days.

Why did I, as other Wiccans, fail to do the grounding process?

For some of us, it may be about getting distracted by the necessities of life—school, work, family responsibilities. For others, it's because a mentor failed to fully train us in grounding techniques.

Many of us may do some forms of grounding but we may

not fully succeed in properly moving the extra energy out of our body.

Now, I'll share three valuable methods of grounding.

1. Eat good food.

Eat something. Carbohydrate rich foods (such as breads or pasta serve) as a good choice because they help pull you down from the high energy state that you achieved during magick working. See my Cakes and Wine Ceremony *in the Appendix* for an example of using food.

2. Push energy into the ground.

Shunt the extra energy back into the earth. One way is to take your hands or bare feet and place them on the bare earth. Release the energy by visualizing that you are pushing the energy into the earth. Mother Earth will recycle it for you. Having any contact with the earth is truly grounding. You can even lie in a field of grass and just deep breathe.

3. Hug a tree.

While hugging a tree, visualize that the extra energy is absorbed by the tree. The tree will do the rest. It naturally helps you pull the energy from your body and restore your internal balance. The tree takes the unneeded energy and shunts the energy down safely into Mother Earth.

* * *

Grounding isn't just for after rituals. Having a tough day at work or school? Ground. Many of us make ourselves sick with built-up, unhealthy energies in our bodies. This can cause headaches and worse.

The solution is to do some grounding. You can release stress by simply deep breathing and placing your feet flat on the ground—no matter where you may be sitting.

Some Wiccans say, "But I am just doing a simple candle spell." You *still* need to ground. You may not be exposed to a whole coven's power, but you still raise energy to do any sort of magick working. This energy needs to be grounded. You may not notice the side-effects at the time, but they will still be there, and they can be harmful.

So if you have completed a ritual or you're just feeling stressed out, *ground*. It not only helps you, but it also helps others.

Now that we see how and why ritual bathing and grounding are so important, here is a spell that you can do to help along in the self love process.

* * * * * *

Your Guide to Casting a Circle

Before any ritual or spell-work, we, Wiccans, cast a circle.

First I'll share some background details. I advise you to cast a sacred circle for all meditations. This way you are safe from entities that may be curious and come to investigate. Also, turn off your electronic goodies for now, making sure you will not be disturbed during your meditation. In addition, you need to be comfortable during the meditation. Make sure your spine is straight. You may want to light a candle.

Next, locate the four directions (north, south, east and west); you can use a compass. Wiccans divide the area of the circle into four parts ("quarters"), corresponding with the four directions. Place the "quarter candles" in their respective corners: green in the northern-most corner, yellow in the east, red in the south, and blue in the west.

Casting circle is important for many reasons. The most important is to contain and concentrate the magick. Another is to protect you from outside forces. Casting circle keeps your efforts concentrated and potent.

Sometimes, people who are new at practicing Wicca feel intimidated when they see some expensive tools for doing rituals.

Popular culture buries us in images of stuff we might want to have. Even in Wiccan circles we see displays of expensive tools for rituals.

What if you see an athame (a black handled knife for casting circle) that is simply stunning in appearance. What if it costs over $500?

The good news is that you do *not* need extra money to buy fancy tools.

Wicca on a Budget

I didn't know what to do. When I first started on the Wiccan path, I read some books and it appeared that I needed a bunch of tools—which I could not afford! What was I to do? Like many young people at that time, I didn't have a lot of money.

Many books don't tell you something important: You probably already have all the tools you need. You don't need all the fancy trappings and trimmings to practice the Craft. Using something simple is just as effective as employing some store-bought, fancy item. Tools encrusted with gems and other trimmings don't make for a better tool.

In fact, the most powerful tools are ones we make ourselves.

Why? As you make the tool, the tool absorbs your energy and so holds more power.

But do not fear if you're not skilled with arts and crafts.

You will do just fine with simple things you gather from within your home. Avoid items made of plastic, though, because they do not hold a magickal charge.

Now, here's a list of things you can use:

Altar: Any table will do.

Altar Cloth: A large square scarf (or even sarong) will work. Just remember that the altar cloth helps to keep wax from damaging the altar. So if you do not want wax on your cloth, find some other material.

Athame: You can use a butter knife. Generally an athame is a black-handled, double edged knife. But a butter knife will work just fine. An athame doesn't need to be sharp. It cuts energy not material things.

Bell: Any bell will work. You can even use a utensil to strike a wine glass. The bell on a cat collar will also work.

Boline: The traditional boline is a white-handled knife often with a curved blade, but a steak knife will work well. This knife, unlike the athame, is used for cutting physical things like herbs. You'll also use the boline to carve runes and names on candles.

Candles: Any kind of candles will do. Further, any inexpensive tea lights would work.

Cauldron: Any fireproof container will do. A pot works well.

Censer: A simple bowl of sand will work just fine.

Goblet or chalice: Any glass will do. A wine glass will work well. Originally, the traditional goblet was made out of wood.

Incense: You could use fresh herbs from your garden if you don't have regular incense.

Offering Dishes: The bowls from your kitchen cabinet will work just fine.

Pentacle: A simple plate painted with a pentagram works. Pentacles were often made out of carved wax, which could be thrown in a fire and melt into nothing. That's one method witches used to stay hidden from the wrath of persecutors.

Salt: It's nice to have sea salt, but the table salt will do.

Wand: A branch from a tree in your garden will work. Make sure it does not touch the ground as this will cause the loss of the power the tree gave it.

Water: You don't need to have spring water. Tap water works fine.

As you can see, most if not all of the tools you need reside in your home already. If you can make your own tools, that's even better. However, most of us are not metalsmiths, nor do we have a forge handy. That's okay, since I shared handy substitute-items above.

Wicca can be done on a budget. All you need is your imagination.

Speaking of imagination, many of us get carried away with the idea of using a Love Spell to "make everything good in our life."

More Details about Sacred Tools

Here are descriptions of the tools Wiccans use for rituals:

• **Athame:** The athame is a ritual dagger, usually double edged with a black handle. The athame is used to consecrate (sanctify) the other elements, such as the salt and water on an altar, and to focus and channel energy. Since it is never used to cut material objects, its blade need not be sharp. The athame is used only to cut energy. The athame is considered a male or phallic symbol.

• **Bell or Chime:** The bell represents the female aspect. When rung, its sound creates a positive energy wave that drives away unwanted entities. It is usually used at the beginning of the ritual to cleanse the space. The bell also can be used as a timing device to signal the next phase of a ritual, for instance, to summon a person into the circle.

• **Besom:** The besom or broom is seen as the sexual union of the God and Goddess. The handle is considered the phallic male symbol that penetrates the bundle of twigs, which is representative of the female vagina. It is used at handfastings (weddings) to not only symbolize fertility but also to exemplify crossing the threshold into a new life together. The besom is also used to clean or sweep away negative energy. You need not actually sweep up dirt to do this; the besom sweeps the negative energies away from a space.

• **Boline:** Unlike the athame, the boline knife has a white handle and is used to actually cut physical things. The boline is sometimes used to scribe letters and symbols on candles for magick work. It is the blade used for physical work.

• **Candles:** Wiccans use candles in many ways. Candles are used to cast spells, to provide lighting, to indicate the

Quarters/directions in a cast circle, and to represent the God and Goddess on the altar.

• **Censer:** There are different kinds of censers (vessels). Depending on the type of incense you use, some hold burning charcoals for raw incense. Others hold cones or sticks of incense, depending on your preference.

• **Cauldron:** Cauldrons come in all shapes and sizes. They are used for making potions as well as for burning incense. Note: Be careful that the cauldron is food-safe since many are made with lead.

• **Cords:** Cords are used to do magick. Some covens use cords to indicate what degree or standing a witch has achieved in his or her coven. Each practitioner has his/her own cords that are worn around the waist.

• **Cup or Chalice:** The cup is a symbol of the womb and is thus a female symbol. It is used to hold sacred wine. During the symbolic Great Rite, an athame is dipped into a chalice filled with wine, blessing it. This act symbolizes the union of the God and Goddess. The wine is then shared among coven members after a portion of the liquid is given to the Gods as an offering.

• **Incense:** When burned, incense is used to purify or charge people and items with energy. It is seen as a male element. Different incense is used for different reasons. One use might be for drawing money toward you.

• **Offering Dishes:** These dishes are used during rituals to set aside offerings to the God and Goddess. They can be made of any material. The choice of design adds a bit of personality to an altar.

• **Pentacle:** The pentacle is a five-pointed star. Each point represents one of the elements (Fire, Water, Air, Earth, and Spirit.) Each element is needed to create life. The pentacle is used to consecrate and or bless material items. It is used as a focal point on an altar.

• **Salt:** Salt is a cleansing element. Since it represents the Earth, salt is seen as feminine. Salt is blessed and placed into water to create consecrated water, which is used to cleanse people, the circle, and the objects used in ritual.

• **Sword:** The sword is generally used to cast the sacred circle. However, if you're in a small room, you can use the athame or a wand. In this way, you avoid accidentally breaking something or hurting someone while using such a large tool. The sword, like the athame, is phallic and therefore a male symbol.

• **Wand:** Like the athame, the wand is used for directing energy. The difference is that the wand is a gentler approach to energy work. You command with an athame, but you invite with a wand. Wands can be used to cast a circle that is semi-permeable.

• **Water:** Water is used in combination with salt. Wiccans use salt to consecrate and purify the water. The salt and water mixture recreates the ocean waters and simulates the salinity of the womb. Water is seen as a feminine element.

Cast the Sacred Circle

Knock three times on the altar. Ring the bell three times.

Light the working candle with the lighter and set the candle down on the altar. (The other candles will be lit from it later using the taper.)

Light the charcoal (if you are using it) from the working candle. (The incense will placed on the charcoal later.)

Take your athame and place its tip into the flame of the working candle. Say:

I exorcise* you, o creature of fire. And I purify and bless you in the names of the Goddess and the God that you are pure and clean.

(*Note: When we speak of *exorcise* here, we are purifying the item by driving out any negative energies.)

Trace a pentacle (a five-pointed star) over the flame. Pick up the candle and raise it up above you and imagine the Gods' energy filling the flame. Place the candle back on the altar.

Take your athame and place its tip into the bowl of water. Say:

I exorcise you, o creature of water. And I purify and bless you in the names of the Goddess and the God that you are pure and clean.

Trace a pentacle in the water. Pick up the bowl of water and raise it up above you and imagine the Gods' energy filling the water. Place the bowl back on the altar.

Take your athame and place its tip into the salt. Say:

I exorcise you, o creature of earth. And I purify and bless you in the names of the Goddess and the God that you are pure and clean.

Trace a pentacle in the salt. Pick up the bowl of salt and raise it up above you and imagine the Gods' energy filling the salt. Place the salt bowl back on the altar.

Take your athame and place its tip into the incense. Say:

I exorcise you, o creature of air. And I purify and bless you in the names of the Goddess and the God that you are pure and clean.

Trace a pentacle over incense. Pick up the incense and raise it up above you and imagine the Gods' energy filling the incense. Place the incense on the lit charcoal.

Take your athame and scoop up three blades of the salt. You may also use your finger. Put the three pinches of salt into the water and mix it with the blade of your athame to make consecrated water. Pick up the bowl of consecrated water and raise it up above you and imagine the Gods' energy filling it.

Take the consecrated water (the salt and water mixture) and dip your fingers into it. Dab some of it on your inner wrists and forehead. Say:

I bless myself with Earth and Water.

Take the censer filled with the burning incense and wave the smoke over you. Say:

I bless myself with Air and Fire.

Take the consecrated water and use your fingers to asperge (sprinkle with consecrated water) the circle boundary. Starting with the north and moving clockwise, walk a complete circle around the perimeter, paying especial attention to aspersing each corner as you go. When finished, place the bowl back on the altar.

Pick up the censer filled with the burning incense. Use your hand to wave the incense smoke around the circle. Starting with north and moving clockwise, walk a complete circle around the perimeter, waving the smoke as you go. Be careful not to burn yourself or anything else. When finished, place the censer back on the altar.

You have just cleansed the space and yourself. Now let's continue by casting the circle.

Take the athame. Envision energy being channeled from you and coming out the tip of your athame [You point the athame outward, away from you as you create the circle.] Starting with north and moving clockwise, walk a complete circle around the perimeter. As you walk, say:

I conjure you, o circle of power, that you be a boundary between the seen mundane world and the spirit world, that you protect me and contain the magick that I shall raise within you! I purify and bless you in the names of the Goddess and the God. So mote it be!

Finish at the east quarter (direction).

Now it's time to "call the quarters." (This refers to the four directions.)

Pick up the athame and the taper from the altar. Light the taper from the working candle. Go and stand in the east corner of where your circle boundary is. Starting with the east candle, say:

I call you up, o mighty ones of the East, element of Air. Come guard my circle and witness my rite.

Trace a pentacle in the air with your athame. Then taking the taper, light the quarter candle for east. Say:

Hail and welcome!

Move clockwise to the south candle. Say:

I call you up, o mighty ones of the South, element of Fire. Come guard my circle and witness my rite.

Trace a pentacle in the air with your athame. Then light the quarter candle for south. Say:

Hail and welcome!

Move clockwise to the west candle. Say:

I call you up, o mighty ones of the West, element of Water. Come guard my circle and witness my rite.

Trace a pentacle in the air with your athame. Then light the quarter candle for west. Say:

Hail and welcome!

Move clockwise to the north candle. Say:

I call you up, o mighty ones of the North, element of Earth. Come guard my circle and witness my rite.

Trace a pentacle in the air with your athame. Then light the quarter candle for north. Say:

Hail and welcome!

Return to the altar. Using the taper, light the Goddess candle, saying:

Welcome, my Lady!

Using the taper, light the God candle, saying:

Welcome, my Lord!

You have now completed casting your circle.

The Self Esteem Ritual

This ritual process will take you seven days. Each day you will meditate on one idea and perform that day's ritual. Repeat the whole ritual for each of the knobs on your *seven day candle* (you can purchase such a candle online). You will need to have your altar or a space for the candle to burn where you can keep it for the week. You will not be burning it continually, just when you are meditating.

Take your seven day candle and consecrate it and bless it (you only need to do this once). Take your boline (a white-handled knife used in circle) and carve on one knob at a time the word or phrase you see below. For example on the top knob carve the word 'Compassion'. On the next or second knob carve 'Peace' and so on until all seven knobs are labeled.

1. Compassion
2. Peace
3. Understanding
4. Serenity
5. Let Go of self doubt
6. Self Worth
7. Self Love

Set the Seven Day knob candle on your altar and then sit in front of it. Light the Seven Day knob candle and say:

Day 1

I ask the Gods to show me the light of their wisdom.

Sit and meditate on the first knob that represents compassion. Ask yourself "how can I be more compassionate to myself?"

Meditate until you have burned the first knob. Then snuff the candle and do the cakes and wine ceremony (see ceremony below).

Day 2

I ask the Gods to show me the light of their wisdom.

Sit and meditate on the second knob that represents peace. Ask yourself "how can I bring more peace to myself?"

Meditate until you have burned the second knob. Then snuff the candle and do the cakes and wine ceremony.

Day 3

I ask the Gods to show me the light of their wisdom.

Sit and meditate on the third knob that represents understanding. Ask yourself "how does compassion and peace help me to understand myself?"

Meditate until you have burned the third knob. Then snuff the candle and do the cakes and wine ceremony.

Day 4

I ask the Gods to show me the light of their wisdom.

Sit and meditate on the fourth knob that represents serenity. Ask yourself "how does understanding myself give me serenity?"

Meditate until you have burned the fourth knob. Then snuff the candle and do the cakes and wine ceremony.

Day 5

I ask the Gods to show me the light of their wisdom.

Sit and meditate on the fifth knob that represents letting go of self doubt. Ask yourself: "How can I let go of self doubt about myself?"

Meditate until you have burned the fifth knob. Then snuff the candle and do the cakes and wine ceremony given later in this chapter.

Day 6

I ask the Gods to show me the light of their wisdom.

Sit and meditate on the sixth knob that represents letting
go of self doubt. Ask yourself: "How do compassion, peace,
understanding, serenity and being able to let go give me self
worth?"

Meditate until you have burned the sixth knob. Then
snuff the candle and do the cakes and wine ceremony.

Day 7

I ask the Gods to show me the light of their wisdom.

Sit and meditate on the seventh knob that represents
letting go of self doubt. Ask yourself: "How am I worthy of
the Gods' love?"

Meditate until you have burned the seventh knob. Then
snuff the candle and do the cakes and wine ceremony.

Cakes and Wine Ceremony

After any ritual, it is important to replenish and ground
your energy. Begin with the wine or juice. Why? When you
do ritual you are using up energy to create your magick
working. You need to feed your body to replace these used
energies. In this way you will stay strong and healthy.

Begin with the wine or juice. Take the cup from your altar
and pour the wine or juice into it. Then take the athame and
dip its tip into the wine or juice. Say:

**As the athame is to the male, so the cup is to the female,
and so joined bring union and harmony.**

Pour some of your blessed wine or juice into the offering
bowl or plate on your altar. Say:

To the Gods!

You can now partake of the beverage.

Take your athame and point it over the cake. Say:

**Blessed be these cakes that they bestow health, peace,
joy, strength, and that fulfillment of love that is perpetual**

happiness.

Take one of the cakes (or just a piece) and place it in the offering bowl or plate. Say:

To the Gods!

You can now partake of the blessed cakes.

So, what do you do with the blessed offerings in the offering dishes? You certainly don't just throw them into the garbage! They are gifts to the Gods. After you close circle take them outside to your garden where you can leave it on the ground to help nourish the Earth.

If you do not have a garden at your home, you can take the offerings out into the woods and leave them there. Some Wiccans who live in the city set the blessed offering out on their porch for local animals to partake. Be sure to only leave biodegradable food. Avoid wrappers or containers that will not decompose.

Closing Circle

It is very important to dismiss the energies you have called for your circle. Be sure to take down the magick temple (circle) you erected. And certainly dismiss the quarters!

To close your circle:

Take your athame and hold it up and stand facing the east. Say:

Hail East, the element of Air. I thank you for guarding my circle and witnessing my rite. May you depart to your fair and lovely realms. I bid you hail and farewell!

Trace a pentacle in the air with your athame.

Continuing, moving in a clockwise circle, stand facing the south. Say:

Hail South, the element of Fire. I thank you for

guarding my circle and witnessing my rite. May you depart to your fair and lovely realms. I bid you hail and farewell!

Trace a pentacle in the air with your athame.

Moving clockwise around the circle, stand facing the west. Say:

Hail West, the element of Water. I thank you for guarding my circle and witnessing my rite. May you depart to your fair and lovely realms. I bid you hail and farewell!

Trace a pentacle in the air with your athame.

Moving clockwise around the circle, stand facing the north. Say:

Hail North, the element of Earth. I thank you for guarding my circle and witnessing my rite. May you depart to your fair and lovely realms. I bid you hail and farewell!

Trace a pentacle in the air with your athame.

Return again to the north, walking clockwise, walk the boundary of the circle, and say:

Fire seal the circle round,

Let it fade beneath the ground,

Let all things be as they once were before.

The circle is now no more,

Merry meet, merry part,

And merry meet again!

So mote it be!

Doing this ritual you will be able to realize and keep the light of the Gods within you always. In my experience the light was always there; I just didn't realize it.

* * * * * *

Special Note About How to Do Rituals throughout this Book:

For Wiccans, we often use a *4-Step Process for Ritual:*
1) Cast the Circle (See Appendix)
2) Do the Specific Ritual
3) Do the Cakes and Wine Ceremony (See Appendix)
4) Close the Circle (See Appendix)

Above on pages 38-46, I showed you the whole 4-Step Process for Ritual.

To avoid any redundancy, I have placed the specific details of Casting the Circle, the Cakes and Wine Ceremony, and Closing the Circle into the **Appendix** of this book.

* * * * * *

The Gods Help with Self Worth

With a new understanding of the Gods' love for me, I began to grow exponentially. Not only did my belief in myself rise, so did my feelings of self worth. The Gods opened my eyes. They gave me the fertile ground in which I could begin to grow. Prior to Their intervention, I was a forgotten seed. But now I had a place to take root.

With the light of the Gods I could now see myself as They saw me.

However, at first it was hard to believe. Growing up, I endured a number of people saying, "You're a fat pig."

This was not true in reality: I was 5 feet 4 inches tall at 112 lbs. But I couldn't perceive myself clearly. I didn't look at myself with love in my heart. I just believed their slander against me.

My brother and even my mother spoon-fed me this unhealthy, untrue belief. And I ate it without hesitation. No wonder I hated my appearance.

Have you noticed how young people are having their

perceptions twisted by damn beauty magazines? The youth are terrified of becoming fat. Researchers note that the majority of 5th grade girls are on diets. What?!

Beauty magazines lie with their photos (which are Photoshopped and enhanced) of models who are really sick and unhealthy. *We were never meant to be skin and bones.*

A number of people point to the BMI index as a good start for considering a weight that may be more appropriate. However, a number of people note that athletic people have denser bodies because of more muscle fibers. So even the BMI index can be off.

Everyone is different. You need to know yourself and what feels right for you. Now I am not advocating that one be overweight. That isn't healthy either. A happy middle ground is best. And each person's middle point is different from everyone else's situation.

About Not Feeling Worthy of the Gods' Love

I'll put this simply. The culture promoted by the mass media and the so-called American values about what is "holy" can truly tear down people.

My Wiccan values are comfortable with the blessing of one's body.

A lot of standard organized religious thinking suggests that the naked body is inherently bad. As a friend who teaches comparative religion shared with me, "This is an old idea of dualism: The body is bad and the spirit is good — which is pushed by certain organized religions."

I now feel fortunate to realize that Wiccan values emphasize that the body is a beautiful gift from the Gods. All sizes are respected and seen as beautiful. The naked body isn't seen as "sinful." The body is a manifestation of the God and Goddess, and therefore, the body is sacred.

Loving partners can share and enjoy each other and their bodies. According to Wicca, the body is *not* merely for reproduction.

I grew up with the idea of an "angry, male God" who found me unworthy at every turn.

Here is the Wiccan truth that I learned: the God and Goddess find me to be worthy!

The Gods have helped me change my viewpoint of how I perceive myself. Instead of looking down on my body, I look at it with respect and gratitude.

The Gods further helped me overcome the lies told to me by my brother and mother. They called me "stupid." Even my father pushed *the lie* that "girls are not good at math."

Fortunately, the Gods taught me that I was *not* the ugly, stupid person I was spoon-fed to believe. The Gods showed me how beautiful and competent I really was. I don't have to be a rocket scientist to be valuable. I was never broken.

Feeling Broken? The Gods Have Your Back.

Have you ever felt broken? Do you question why you are the way you are because you don't look "normal" or you can't do the same activities as the "normal people" do?

I'm here to tell you that you were made the way you're *supposed* to be. Even with the so-called "flaws."

We all feel we have flaws. Yes, they can feel so painful to live with. We suffer—emotionally or physically—sometimes we suffer both ways. It's hard to endure.

I have dyslexia *and* depression. Why, I wondered, did the Gods make me broken?

But I didn't realize that the Gods did NOT make a mistake. I have what people call disabilities. However, I've learned something startling. They're not disabilities. I call them *enhancements*.

How the hell could dyslexia *plus* depression be enhancements? I had to dig deep and realize that these enhancements *create the opportunity* to grow exponentially. These enhancements help us grow in ways that others can't because they have not had to face the struggle, the pain and . . . the *rise* from the ashes.

Dyslexia had been my curse. But, unlike others, I had to fight and press on through headaches to read the books I've read. However, this has made me stronger. Now have a tenacity that a number of my friends do *not* have.

Depression had me cutting myself years ago. Depression had me doubt that I had any worth at all. It took therapy, the Gods' guidance, and the love of my sweetheart to encourage me and show me I wasn't dirt. Depression was wrong! I have learned that I am NOT a depressed person. I am a Spirit anointed by the Gods, a Spirit who deals with depression symptoms. That's a BIG difference! Simply it's a choice. What do you choose? Making your own decisions to take root in your life is a good place to start.

Now, my friend, I want to ask you two heartfelt questions.

- *Where do you feel broken?*
- *And how could your flaws or disabilities be a road so that you can rise up a stronger, deeper, more blessed person than ever before?*

You might want to meditate on your *enhancement(s)* and see how they have positively affected your life and what they have taught you. Consider writing about this in your personal journal. *Learn to change your personal story.* Empower yourself by identifying how your enhancements have given you the opportunities to become stronger and deeper.

Along the lines of changing your personal story, you can use a personal metaphor. In this next section, we're going to use the metaphor of a redwood tree.

What Can a Redwood Tree Teach Us about Life and Wicca?

Have you noticed that certain small things can grow much larger in your life? Think of a seed that eventually grows into a mighty redwood tree.

Decisions are like seeds. They have the potential to grow into something so much bigger.

I remember an important seed in my life: my decision to learn about one particular word—Wicca. From there I grew in my practice to become a Wiccan High Priestess.

My first decision, like a seed, grew into my life's path.

Think about your decisions. What have you grown in your life?

Further, imagine looking at a cross section of a redwood tree. You'll notice the rings of the tree that reveal its lifecycle.

Now, think of these rings as different layers just like your life has different layers or stages.

At each "ring" or life stage, we're making new decisions.

Some decisions make us resilient like a redwood tree. When there's a fire in a forest, a tree may be damaged. After the trauma has passed, the redwood tree may bear the scars. But this tree can bounce back and become bigger and mightier than before.

You can, too! In Wicca, we use the tools of meditation and the Gods' guidance to become that mighty redwood.

A few days ago, I went camping among redwood trees. A park ranger told me that the cones of a redwood tree need the heat of a forest fire in order to open and release their seeds. What a vivid image. Trauma can create a new life path.

A major trauma in your life can create new growth for you personally. With each wrong choice or even a disaster, we have the potential to grow to our mightiest form because we learn from those mistakes.

Redwood trees teach us much about personal growth, and they can teach us a great deal more.

One thing we all need to learn about is dealing with stress.

The Gods and Helping with Stress

Have you recently had to make some choices that brought you stress?

Stress can tell us a lot. We can see what is important to us. In this way, stress can actually guide us to the secrets of our hearts. How? We wouldn't be feeling stressed out about something if we didn't think it was important and being threatened.

Once we know what we value, we can better set our course through life.

You see, what we need is clarity.

This is where the Gods can help. If you're under pressure and feeling the burden of stress, you can ask the Gods for clarity.

Why is clarity so important? When you can see things clearly, you can make a plan and take appropriate action. Those two things will reduce your stress.

One of the best ways to do that is through meditation. Here is a simple meditation to ask the Gods for their guidance.

For all meditations, follow these simple guidelines.

- Find a place where you will not be disturbed for the entire meditation.

- Turn off the ringer of your cell phone.
- Take a sitting position where your spine is straight and your feet are flat on the floor.
- Dim the lights.

This meditation is really great for asking for guidance from the Gods. If you are having problems and are unclear as to what you need to do next I highly recommend this meditation.

To effectively conduct this meditation, it's best for you to sit quietly and to *hear* the guiding words (the words in boldface below). You have two options for you to hear such words:

a) Before you meditate, use a recording device and record the guiding words (for later playback).

OR

b) Have a friend (or loved one), read this portion of the book out loud to you. (In this way, this person serves as the facilitator of your guided meditation).

1) Cast the Circle (see the Appendix)
2) *Guidance Meditation*
Start by closing your eyes.
Begin breathing in and out deeply.
With each breath in, you pull in relaxation.
With each breath out, you release the stresses of the day.

(short pause)

And as you keep breathing in and out deeply,
Notice now that the light begins to fade around you.
Slowly at first, it gets darker and darker.
Until you are in total darkness, where you feel safe and

secure in the darkness.

(short pause)

Then, just as the darkness came, it leaves.

A new light blooms around you, slowly at first, but gradually it gets brighter and brighter.

You see you are in the middle of a circle of standing stones. The great henge, it protects you from all bad entities.

There is a large stone altar in the middle of the great henge. You go to it and sit in front of the altar.

Closing your eyes, you ask the Gods for their guidance.

As you sit, you now notice two loving energies beside you.

One is the Goddess and one is the God.

You ask them for their help and they lovingly answer your request.

(long pause for listening)

Now that you have received Their guidance They bid you farewell.

Your time here is now done and it is time to return from where you came.

You again notice the light starts to dim, slowly at first, it gets darker and darker.

Until you are in total darkness, where you feel safe and secure in the darkness.

(short pause)

Then, just as the darkness came, it leaves.

A familiar light returns, slowly at first, but gradually it gets brighter and brighter.

Until the light is back and you now can see you are back in the room and safe.

3) Conduct the Cakes and Wine Ceremony (see the Appendix).

4) Close the Circle (see the Appendix)

* * *

With the Gods' help, you can move towards happiness in your life by making the best decisions for yourself. Ultimately, making excellent decisions reduces your stress level. Further, you'll feel less stress because you know that you're receiving guidance from the Gods.

The Gods are always there to help you. All you need is to ask for their help. You can go to them for anything that you need help on.

Knowing this now, what guidance would you ask the Gods for?

An important part of interacting with the Gods includes expressing and feeling gratitude.

Remember to be Thankful

It's so easy to forget the blessings in our lives. They happen everyday. Some may be small, but they are there. However, many of us only remember the things that troubled us during the day.

It's like a stubbed toe that screams "pay attention." But we miss acknowledging all the other toes that are just fine. We concentrate on that which gives us pain.

But what about the joys in our day? The cat that purrs

with affection as you caress it; your partner's smile in the morning; and hearing your favorite song on the radio. How about when your loved one makes your favorite meal?

I invite you to push forward the joys and blessing of your day. Pause. Pay attention. Push the "stubbed toe" into the background.

How do we push the joys and blessings forward? Write in your gratitude journal. What's a gratitude journal? It is a journal in which you record the day's blessings you are grateful for. Let's think about your day in a different way. Sometimes, I think of a day as glancing out a window and seeing two things: a pile of garbage next to a glorious rose. When you write in your gratitude journal, you're looking at the rose.

When I write down the "roses" of my day, I'm always surprised about how many that actually occurred.

How about you? How many positive things are in your life right now? You're reading this, so your eyes are working. You're breathing. You're probably looking forward to something even, perhaps a favorite TV show.

I find that consciously choosing to look at the "roses" of life helps me focus on the beauty and joy that I experience. Soon after I started writing in my gratitude journal, I realized that I didn't just have one rose; I really had a rose garden.

Now, you can take this a step further. In addition to remembering the roses of your life, show your gratitude. Do a simple ritual at the end of your day. After noting my blessings in my gratitude journal, I take a candle and offer it as thanks to the Gods for the blessings I enjoyed.

Tea light candles work great for this. They are small and don't take too long to burn. This way you don't have a candle burning when no one is around. (Never leave a burning candle unattended.)

This candle is a small gesture to the Gods in thanks for all the blessings they provide. Since starting this ritual, I have noticed even more blessings occurring in my life.

The nice thing about this ritual is that it doesn't take much time and it doesn't require a big fanfare. As long as your ritual is heartfelt and sincere the Gods will be pleased.

If you live with someone who isn't Wiccan, lighting a candle is not a big inconvenience. Simply let them know that this is a positive part of your daily life. Make sure that you never leave a burning candle unattended, though.

This ritual is a great way to say "I noticed" and "thanks" to the Gods. They will appreciate it. This ritual also helps you be happier and healthier.

CHAPTER 3:
THE GODS HELP YOU SOLVE PROBLEMS

Do you get tired of facing problems day in and day out? Fortunately, the Gods welcome us to ask for help with problems. In fact, this is tied in with one of my favorite phrases "Goddess Has Your Back" which my sweetheart devised.

Let's begin . . .

The Gods and Helping with the Perspective of Prejudice

Have you experienced prejudice in your life? Was it because you were Wiccan or pagan?

Prejudice can take many forms. But what do you do when it happens?

First, assess the situation. Can you educate the offending person? I have been in situations when the offending person thinks he's right and will hear nothing that differs from his beliefs.

Make sure no one is being harmed. There is a big

difference between offensive words and physical violence. You may need to take action. Maybe you need to quickly get to a place of safety. You might even have to call 911 for police intervention.

Take care of your own feelings. Before I get caught up in an aggression tornado, I remember to simply breathe. Concentrating on your breath is a great way to help yourself calm down. Then you can take control of the words that come out of your mouth. You can't control what they say, but you can control what you say and do.

Find your way to compassion. The Gods and Goddesses love their children (all of them) so become the Goddess in her nurturing state. Let her energy flow within you. Let the Goddess help you select your words. Avoid words that sting; instead say something constructive and nurturing to the conversation. How would this sound? One way to respond is: "I heard what you said. That's not what my life is about. I'm leaving this room."

When I say compassion, I do not mean let them walk all over you. The idea is to make space in yourself to understand those who are ignorant of your beliefs. They don't know what they are talking about. To take their words personally gives them power. Do not let that happen. Do not give these untruths any power.

Renew yourself. Once the incident is over, take some time to do a Breathing Meditation. I know how much it helps to salve the wounds their words have left.

How do the Gods help in all this? Through your breathing Meditation (below) you can ask the Gods to help you have compassion for yourself and the offender. This doesn't excuse the offender; this is intended to give you peace.

(Again, you have a choice: you can record the following

words for later playback . . . or . . . you can have a friend say them out loud to guide you through the meditation.)

1) Cast the Circle (see the Appendix)
2) *Breathing In the Gods Meditation*
Start by closing your eyes.
Begin breathing in and out deeply.
With each breath in, you pull in relaxation.
With each breath out, you release the stresses of the incident.
And as you keep breathing in and out deeply,
You can now feel the compassion from the Gods fill your lungs with each inhale.
Taking this compassion in, you can have compassion, both for yourself and also for the instigator.

(long pause for breathing in compassion)

Now that you have soaked up as much of the Gods' compassion as you can, you can take a deep breath in and open your eyes.

3) Do the Cakes and Wine Ceremony (see Appendix)
4) Close the Circle (see Appendix)

* * *

I keep this light and this understanding of compassion within me at all times. Sometimes it's hard to see it, but it is always there. With self-love and compassion, we can manifest anything we wish. From the foundation of self-love, we have the energy and personal peace from which we can help others on their path. This helps me have the compassion I need for myself and for others.

What happens when you come across other problems? How do you deal with them?

Problems Are Like Piñatas

How could a problem be like a piñata? Problems seem to come out of nowhere. At times we swing at them with seemingly no effect. It can feel like we're blindfolded.

The truth is: the Gods have hidden secret goodies inside of problems. Lessons and blessings are packed inside problems, just like candy and small gifts are inside piñatas. We just need to know that the goodies are there and how to see them.

To solve a problem, keep swinging at it. However, a problem (piñata) doesn't stay still. And that's akin to a problem that is hard to solve. We may have to extend a lot of effort to solve a particular problem.

Just when I think I'm about to solve it, the problem evolves or moves to a different level of complexity. Just like piñatas rise or fall to different positions. The little buggers can move on you.

So how do you solve the piñata or problem? With a bat or stick, of course.

We use different tools in our lives to solve our problems. Sometimes we use magick, but many times we use mundane or ordinary actions. We can use a combination of the two. Sometimes we need the Gods' help to swing our bat. As Wiccans we have many bats to choose from.

First, I employ mundane actions to solve a problem. If that fails, I get a different bat, magick. Since magick comes in many forms, it's like having a bunch of bats to choose from.

You can call on the Gods for particularly tough problems. The Gods won't solve your problems for you, but they will guide you. They help you aim your bat at your piñata. The Gods also teach us how to extract the knowledge that is within the problem.

Many swings may be necessary to solve a problem to receive the insights, blessings and lessons within. Once you solve the problem or open the piñata, you can partake of the blessings.

Sometimes we have a hard time telling which parts are the prize and which are not. When blessings and lessons are obscured, you can ask the Gods for insights through meditation.

Some problems are packed full of blessings in disguise. Others contain just a few nuggets of wisdom. However, all are valuable in our growth. I've noticed that the harder it is to acquire the goodies, the better they usually are. But not always.

Life comes with many piñatas. When we step into a new stage of life, a piñata gives us new challenges and gifts. In this process, we can continue stepping up our knowledge and understanding of our world and our lives. One tool I use to solve problems is what I call a *Pattern-Affirmation.*

How You Can Use Something Better Than an Affirmation

What do you want? Have you tried to coach yourself to change your own behavior?

Some people attempt to push themselves with statements like: "I'm a thin person."

Well, I'll tell you the truth. When I tell myself, "I'm a thin person," my brain yells at me: "Oh, yeah! Look in the mirror!"

The phrase "I'm a thin person" is called an *affirmation.* In essence, a person tries to "affirm" something that currently is not true.

No wonder so many people say, "Affirmations don't work for me."

This bothered me, so I came up with some new ideas before I gave one of my workshops. The tool I created is a Pattern-Affirmation. (In discussion with my friend Tom Marcoux, he gave me two labels "Pattern-Affirmation" and "Wish-Affirmation" to add to my thoughts).

In essence, a Wish-Affirmation is truly a *standard* affirmation that people try to use, often with disappointing results.

A Wish-Affirmation is: "I'm a thin person."

On the other hand, a Pattern-Affirmation is "I eat like a 130 lb. person." Or better yet "I have a lifestyle of a 130 lb. person."

Do you see the distinction?

A Wish-Affirmation is something you aspire to.

Instead, a Pattern-Affirmation is something that *can be true right away.* You can exhibit a different behavior now. Your very next action can contribute to your healthy lifestyle.

You can even apply the Pattern-Affirmation process to having financial abundance.

For example, a Wish-Affirmation could be "I am wealthy." On the other hand, a Pattern-Affirmation could be: "I'm careful with my personal budget like a prosperous person."

In this way you will have more success in achieving your desires on a day-to-day basis. Now, I'll share a helpful process.

The Pattern-Affirmation Ritual

Here are the steps:

1. Gather a Seven Day Candle and a Circle Script.
2. Pick your Pattern-Affirmation.
3. Do the Pattern-Affirmation Ritual.

The process is as follows:

First, be sure to pick a suitable Pattern-Affirmation. Remember, it needs to address a pattern of behavior you want to instill.

Here are examples:

*   I eat like a 130 lb. person
*   I study one hour a day like a good student.
*   I listen to my daughter's thoughts and feelings like a good father.

1) Cast the Circle (see Appendix)

2) *Pattern-Affirmation Ritual*

Do the daily candle meditation as described below.

Note: On each day you first Cast the Circle, then do the visualization and meditation. Then do the Cakes and Wine Ceremony and finally Close the Circle.

Day1

Take the candle and place it on your altar. Say aloud your Pattern-Affirmation as you light the candle. Visualize that you're guiding energy into the candle.

Meditate on your Pattern-Affirmation for five minutes or more until the first knob is burned down.

Day 2

Take the candle and place it on your altar. Say aloud your Pattern-Affirmation as you light the candle. Visualize that you're guiding energy into the candle.

Meditate on your Pattern-Affirmation for five minutes or more until the second knob is burned down.

Day 3

Take the candle and place it on your altar. Say aloud your Pattern-Affirmation as you light the candle. Visualize that you're guiding energy into the candle.

Meditate on your Pattern-Affirmation for five minutes or more until the third knob is burned down.

Day 4

Take the candle and place it on your altar. Say aloud your Pattern-Affirmation as you light the candle. Visualize that you're guiding energy into the candle.

Meditate on your Pattern-Affirmation for five minutes or more until the fourth knob is burned down.

Day 5

Take the candle and place it on your altar. Say aloud your Pattern-Affirmation as you light the candle. Visualize that you're guiding energy into the candle.

Meditate on your Pattern-Affirmation for five minutes or more until the fifth knob is burned down.

Day 6

Take the candle and place it on your altar. Say aloud your Pattern-Affirmation as you light the candle. Visualize that you're guiding energy into the candle.

Meditate on your Pattern-Affirmation for five minutes or more until the sixth knob is burned down.

Day 7

Take the candle and place it on your altar. Say aloud your Pattern-Affirmation as you light the candle. Visualize that you're guiding energy into the candle.

Meditate on your Pattern-Affirmation for five minutes or more until the seventh knob is burned down.

3) Do the Cakes and Wine Ceremony (see Appendix)
4) Close the Circle (see Appendix)

* * *

Using this new tool of a Pattern-Affirmation Ritual, you will grow in new and exciting ways.

Now, we'll move on to Knot Magick.

Knot Magick

Want to do a simple spell that could help you get a job, heal from an illness or provide you prolonged protection on a trip? The answer is knot magick (also known as *cord magick*). This form of magick working has been used for centuries in everything from weaving carpets to knitting and crocheting.

Better yet, you can simply make one knot to accomplish knot magick. This process requires no obscure objects or substances to acquire. You can do knot magick anywhere and at anytime.

So what do you use for tying the knots?

First, use natural substances because they hold a magickal charge, while synthetics do not. Use cotton, silk or other natural fibers for your knot magick, and this choice will help you succeed.

Use each cord only once. Blending intentions weakens and can even pollute your magick.

How to do knot magick

The first step is to identify specifically what you want to do.

Some examples are:

- Get a job
- Heal
- Arrange protection

Wiccans use knot magic in two ways: the Proactive approach and the Reactive approach.

Proactive means preparing ahead of time. Imagine that it's two weeks before hurricane season. You go to stores for supplies and for materials to board up your house or business.

On the other hand, *Reactive* means you rush around during the storm and try to live through it.

Most knot magick is done *proactively*. You prepare ahead of time so that your magick can improve a situation or even prevent trouble.

Historically, sailors asked witches to place the winds into knots so that the sailors would have a remedy if they were stuck in a dead calm. They would untie one of the knots to make the winds blow.

The Steps of Knot Magick

One of the most important things in your magick is *will*. You need it to successfully fuel your spell. What exactly is will? Will means the *driving force of desire for some form of change*. So I focus on the power of "I will." This is an important distinction because many people think of willpower as only the ability to avoid temptation.

Secondly, you must believe! If you do not believe, then your magick will falter.

Finally, master Pranic Breathing, also known as belly breathing. If you're familiar with yoga, you probably know of Pranic Breathing techniques.

In Pranic Breathing, you breathe in deeply extending the stomach, utilizing all of your lung capacity. Visualize pulling up energy from the earth. Through Pranic Breathing, you move energy. Visualize your breath as a colored mist.* This mist will carry *your will* and your intention into the knot. (This process is also referred to as "the breath of life.")

* Note: You can imagine your breath as a greenish-blue mist. You can also visualize it as different colors depending on your intention. For example, you could focus on the color orange for more confidence for a job interview.

Now, let's go through the steps in order:
1. Figure out what you need, that is, your intention.
2. Start tying a knot into your cord (do not tighten it yet) and simultaneously, focus *your will* on your intention.
3. Do Pranic Breathing.
4. Have your desire firmly fixed in your mind. Know it as reality, even for just a moment. At that point, blow your will (your breath in the form of a colored mist) into the knot and *tighten it closed.*
5. When you have completed the process, engage in *grounding* yourself.

You have just completed knot magick.

In knot magick, Wiccans usually work in odd numbers: tying five, seven or nine knots in the cord.

The order in which you tie the knots is also important. Please view the correct order in this image here:

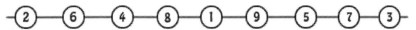

As you tie each knot you recite a line of the following poem. This poem is designed for tying nine knots.

Knot Magick Chant
By knot of one, the spell has begun,
By knot of two, my words become true,
By knot of three, it comes to me,
By knot of four, I've opened the door,
By knot of five, this spell's alive,
By knot of six, this spell is fixed,
By knot of seven, there is no question,
By knot of eight, it's now my fate,
By knot of nine, this thing's now mine!
So mote it be.

Recently, I used knot magick before I attended a vital meeting. Just knowing that I worked knot magick relieved some of my stress. Of course, I still had to do the mundane work of gathering materials and rehearsing my words for the meeting.

But it was a relief to know that I had invoked the blessings of the Gods, too.

I invite you to consider knot magick to help your life.

Knot magick can be really useful in a pinch when you need something right away.

CHAPTER 4:
THE GODS AND RELATIONSHIPS

How can the Gods help us have healthy relationships? First, They guide us through Their own example. Theirs is a loving and respectful relationship. The God having superior physical strength lays his strength at the feet of the Goddess, for she has great wisdom. They work together. Even though the God could overpower the Goddess physically, he knows that she has the nurturing compassion to use his strength wisely.

They work together and support each other for the good of their children and the universe. This creates a loving healthy relationship between them. Healthy relationships in our own lives work in the same way. We need to respect each other and work together. Just like the God respects the Goddess and lays down his strength to her, trusting her wisdom to use it wisely, each person must respect the other to have a healthy relationship.

Just as the God and Goddess each have their own strengths and work together for the betterment of each other, we need to bring love and support.

But what happens when things go wrong? Years ago, I found myself in an abusive marriage. So I turned to the Gods and They helped me gain the strength to get a divorce. But I still wasn't completely separated from the guy. I still had the astral bonds that we had woven together during our marriage. So I created a ritual to completely separate myself from this relationship and all its energy-tethers.

How to Heal by Separating Yourself Spiritually from a Bad Relationship

We've all been in a bad relationship at some time in our lives—whether it is a family problem or ex-lovers or a friendship that just plain went sour. So how do we spiritually separate ourselves from these poisonous people?

You can use many different ways to accomplish this. However, the first and foremost thing to do is to verbally end the relationship. You might say something like: "I don't think this is healthy for us. So let's just stop seeing each other."

Second, physically stay away from the person. The idea is to stop spiritually ingesting the poison of interacting with them. (You also need to stop phone calls, texts, and social media interactions, too.)

Many people hesitate to do the first two steps. For many, true change is quite difficult. I can relate to this. And, I'm providing the ritual below for when you're truly ready to move on with your life.

Now, it's time to use what I call the *Separation Ritual*. This ritual involves disconnecting the astral connections that you and the person made during the relationship.

Unless you take action, you stay connected to the person. How? Your astral bodies remain connected. Negative energy can still be transferred both ways. To protect yourself from these bad energies you must cut all ties from that person. This is where the Separation Ritual comes in.

Ideally, the person would participate in a Separation Ritual with you. That often does *not* happen. So you take an object that will *stand in* for the person. This object could be a picture or even a teddy bear, if the person likes teddy bears.

Use a long piece of red yarn or red string, which represents the connections you have between you and the toxic person. Red is for the life force but you can uses another color if you think that would be a better representation.

For this ritual you'll need both your athame (to cast your circle) and a *boline,* which is a white handle knife used specifically for cutting physical objects during ritual.

Important: Athames are used to cut *energy.* Bolines are used to cut *physical objects.*

Here are the steps of True Separation:
1. Verbally end the relationship
2. Stay away from the person.
3. Ground yourself.
4. Cast circle.
5. Do the Separation Ritual (see below).
6. Do the Cakes and Wine ritual.
7. Close the circle.
8. Finally continue to have no contact with the toxic person.

With this rite you will be able to move forward with your life. It can help you get past bad feelings about a bad relationship.

You will need your usual ritual items to cast circle and

your altar. As I mentioned you will also have an object that represents the person and a long piece of red yarn or red string. The yarn/string must be long enough to encircle your own waist and to encircle the object that represents the toxic person.

1) Cast the Circle (See Appendix)
2) *The Separation Ritual*
Take the object that represents the person from whom you are separating. First, you will asperge it. *Asperge* means to sprinkle the holy water onto the object with your fingers.

With the holy water, asperge and say:
I cleanse and consecrate you by water and earth.

Next you will cense the object. *Cense* means to waft incense smoke over the object.

With the incense smoke, cense and say:
I bless and charge you with air and fire.

Then take the yarn/string and cense and asperge it as well and say:
I cleanse and consecrate you by water and earth.

Next you will cense the yarn/string. Cense means to waft incense smoke over the string/yarn.

With the incense smoke, cense and say:
I bless and charge you with air and fire.

Take the red yarn/string in your hands, and say:
Tiny bundle of yarn/string
You are now the same as the bonds between me and (Name of person.)

Tie one end of the yarn/string to the object and then encircle your waist with the other end of the yarn/string, while you say:

You *are* the bonds that connect us now.
From me to (Name of person) and from (Name of

person) to me.

Our connection is by thee.

Sit and concentrate on the bond between you both and see it as the yarn/string that now connects you and the object. Once you have a firm connection with that thought, take the boline and cut the yarn/string, seeing in your mind's eye the astral bonds being cut along with the yarn/string.

Once you complete the cut, say:

I am now free of the ties of (Name of person) as he/she is of me.

May my happiness expand, and may (Name of person's) happiness expand.

Blessed be.

3) Do the Cakes and Wine Ceremony (See Appendix)

4) Close the Circle (See Appendix)

Separating ourselves from toxic people is important for our happiness and well being. It even blesses the life of the other person. You are doing yourself and the other person a favor.

I trust that this ritual will help you be happier and healthier.

* * * * * *

Many of us have relationships with animals as our loving companions. My cat Magick comforts me when I'm down, picks me up from a bad mood, and keeps me company when I am lonely. Magick loves me for who I am (especially when I feed him).

Magick comforts me when others can't and is always waiting for me at home.

Our relationship began at the shelter where I always adopt a new furry friend. I went in to find a cat to be my companion. While I was looking at some cute tabbies, I saw these two little eyes staring out from a cubbyhole. Then the eyes came closer as this little black kitten slipped out, moving confidently towards me. He greeted me and sat in front of me almost saying, "Okay Mom, let's go home."

That was when the shelter volunteer said, "Oh, the black ones never get adopted."

What witch could say no to that! I took him home that same day. I named him Magick and he has been my little loving friend ever since. This leads us to the topic of a witch's familiar.

Time for a Wiccan's Familiar?

About three years ago, a particular witch held a ritual in the woods each weekend. To her delight, a certain deer joined her each time. When I heard about this, I realized one can have a wild animal as a *familiar*—an animal, usually a pet, that helps the witch.

At one point, I was in a Wiccan learning group gathered in the woods when an owl joined us. Animals sense energy which makes them good working partners.

Animals are so proficient at using energy that they can literally move in and out of a closed circle and not harm or break that circle. So when your familiar moves across the boundary of your cast circle don't worry; they won't hurt it.

Small children can also cross your circle's boundary without disturbing it. It's only when we get older that we become unable to do that. The reason? Society teaches us to limit ourselves and so we unconsciously do so.

On the other hand, familiars do not have that burden. They can move and work energy in ways that many of us cannot. This is why witches and other magick users like to have a familiar.

However, don't just run to an animal shelter and pick any animal and assume that the little one will be your familiar. *An animal must choose to do so.* If your little friend does not make that choice of being a familiar, you can just enjoy the company of your pet in ordinary life.

So how can I tell if my pet or another animal wants to be my familiar? Observe: Does the animal want to hang around you as you do a ritual? When you ground and center does your cat (for example) come and sit, to support you?

If you observe a particular animal in the wild repeatedly showing up during your rituals, pause. Ask yourself, "Does this one want to be my familiar or is this just a random visit?" (**Note:** This does **not** mean that you go over and pet the animal. They do **not** want that. You can nod in the animal's direction as a greeting.)

Sometimes, you may discover that this particular animal *is* quietly acting as a familiar for you.

Note: Never try to force an animal to work with you. If you have a pet, but the little one just strolls away when you're doing a ritual, let it go. Just love your pet for the other joyful moments you share. You do *not* need a familiar.

If you, at some time, find an animal that wants to work with you, it can be quite rewarding. (The familiar sends energy to your spell-work.) Not only will your spells and other workings be more powerful, but you will also have a great friend by your side.

What a joyful experience.

* * *

Over the course of your relationship with an animal, you

will arrive at a tough time. How do you honor your furry friend?

Is it Time to Let Go or Time to Hold Fast?

Cleo, my cat, looked up at me. At 14 years old, Cleo needed me to give her intravenous fluids to sustain her. One night while I was administering her daily fluids she simply looked into my eyes and told me, *I've had enough, I'm done.*

I just *knew.* Other times, I've wrestled with the decision of when it was time to let go of my beloved pet.

Now, I've had cats my whole life. In high school, I was introduced to domesticated, pet rats. These little furry friends have terribly short life spans. I'd have four at the same time, and this meant crying every year as one of them would become ill due to old age. I had many times to practice letting go.

I have spent thousands of dollars for medical care for my fuzzy babies. But how does one know when to let go?

If a pet or familiar is close to crossing the veil, when is it truly time to let go?

First listen to your little friend. Here are some signs to help you consider when to let go:

- Is your furry companion still interested in life?
- Does your companion still enjoy eating?
- Does he/she still play in spite of the illness or disease?
- Is the little one in tremendous pain that prevents him/her from being happy?

Now I'm not talking about temporary illness. This is about the end of a life—a terminal illness.

Recently, on Facebook, people discussed the condition of Blacky, The Wheelchair Cat.

A native of New Zealand, he has one eye, and after being struck by a car, he's left with spinal nerve damage and paralysis in his rear legs and bladder.

A number of people suggested that Blacky be "put down."

But wait a moment! Blacky can now feel his legs if one tickles them. Sometimes he moves or stands on them. Last year, he had a perianal urethrostomy surgery because of his bladder problems.

Still, Blacky enjoys life. He enjoys going outside and playing. Other than his mobility issue, Blacky's now healthy.

In summary, I invite you to look at my list and let it help you make a good decision about whether it may be time to let a pet go.

Sure, sometimes our pets have physical troubles. But you've probably noticed that we humans can have physical troubles, too. Still, we find ways to have joy and meaning.

Let's make sure to support our furry friends in their times of need.

* * *

We have talked about relationships with people and with animals, but what about the Gods? How do we build good relationships with Them?

The good news is that much of this book shows you exactly how to honor the Gods and to express your appreciation for Their kindness to you.

Some Wiccans experience tough times and feel that they must have offended the Gods. They wail, "Why did this bad thing happen to me? If the Gods love me why do they let me suffer?"

Why Do Bad Things Happen?

I can't breathe. I'm in the Emergency Room area, waiting. But they're not taking me in. They're leaving me in the waiting room.

That's how I felt a few days ago. It was my second time in the hospital in 24 hours. There's no other word for it: *suffering*. I felt a big weight on my chest, preventing me from taking in an adequate breath.

In my suffering, some thoughts rose up. *Why are the Gods letting this happen to me? Haven't I been serving Their plan well enough?*

Can you relate to this? Perhaps, you're suffering now. Or you've suffered in the recent past. It's hard to reconcile a vision of the Gods' love for us with the suffering we endure.

There's a secret that I want to share with you. The Gods *do* love us. And in this divine love they know that we've signed up for a life in which we grow. The tough truth is: suffering is part of our path of learning and becoming who we truly are.

Suffering forms us and sculpts us through the experiences we go through, both good and bad.

You may say: "I didn't ask for this."

Maybe not, but you do want something—the freedom to become what you *can* become. We incarnate in bodies that can manifest, at times, as fragile. Difficult times will happen. How we participate in life (including suffering) shapes us.

For example, I don't want to experience pain related to clinical depression, but that's something I deal with. This experience gives me a whole different viewpoint.

In recent days, I've been dealing with a whole new, terrible burden: extreme asthma. When I can't breathe, I feel like I'm dying. That gives me a *different* perspective.

I'll tell you one gift that comes with both clinical depression and extreme asthma: compassion. I feel great compassion for people who have these burdens—and other people who have heavy burdens.

As Wiccans, we do have an advantage when dealing with suffering. Our faith can sustain us. We can know that the Gods are present to support us as we travel our path, especially when we're suffering.

Call upon the Gods. Do ritual. Feel your divine connection.

The Gods are rooting for you. They are here to help guide you through these events. They support you in your times of need. They celebrate in your times of triumph.

Just remember the Gods are here for you and are always by your side—even when you don't see it.

They are our cheerleaders and our coaches in life. They teach by example and with love.

To develop a relationship with a particular God or Goddess, do some research about Him or Her. After your research, the next step is to meditate.

How does one meditate? Set up a time and place where you will not be disturbed. You can have items set up in front of you that a particular deity likes.

The following meditation starts in the Witch's Cottage, a safe place where it is best to start your meditations. Your cottage is a place of protection, where only you can enter. It's a place of security and peace.

Witch's Cottage Meditation
1) Cast the Circle (see Appendix)
Note: This meditation includes special pauses. During a pause you have the time to interact with the environment of the Witch's Cottage on the astral plane. (As with other guided meditations in this book, consider either having a friend read the directions to you or pre-recording the

material in your own voice for later playback.) When you come across the words "Short pause" do not say them aloud. Simply pause before you move onward.

2) *Witch's Cottage Meditation*

Relax. Take a deep breath in. Breathe out, releasing the stresses of the day. Keep taking deep breaths, in and out. With each exhale you get more and more relaxed. Feel your body as it sits comfortably Notice now that the light slowly begins to dim. You feel comfortable and at peace as the light continues to fade. Now the light is gone and you are happy and secure in the darkness.

(Short pause)

Soon you notice the light starts to return. Slowly at first. Then as your eyes adjust to the new light, you now can see that you are in a Cottage. The air is fresh and clean. Look around to orient yourself to your new surroundings. Look to the south wall and see a warm, friendly fire crackling in a large stone fireplace. Walk to the fireplace and enjoy the light and warmth the fire gives you. Observe the fireplace What kind of stone is it made of? What kind of kindling is being used?

(1 minute pause)

Look to your right and notice the west wall and then walk to it and see a nearby fountain. What does this fountain look like? How was it constructed?

(1 minute pause)

Look to your right and see the north wall and walk to it. Near the wall is a large stone table. Observe the table. What distinguishing marks does it have?

(1 minute pause)

Turn to your right again and view the east wall. Walk to it and now see a well-kept window set into the wall. What can you see out of the window? What time of day or night is it?

(1 minute pause)

Further explore the cottage. What does it smell like? What materials were used in its construction? How many rooms do you see?

(5 minutes pause)

Find a nice place to sit. Rest a while. Then notice how the light starts dimming. Feel comfortable and at peace as the light continues to fade. Now the light is gone and you are happy and secure in the darkness.

(Short Pause)

Soon you notice that the light starts to return. Slowly at first. Your eyes adjust to the new light and you feel safe, calm and refreshed. Now open your eyes to your present-day world.

3) Do the Cakes and Wine Ceremony (See Appendix)
4) Close the Circle (See Appendix)

Now that we have established your own Witch's Cottage, we can begin the introduction process to different deities.

Before you meet the God in the following meditation, you will first interact with the Guardian, the protector of the doorway to the Witch's Cottage. This Guardian can be anyone that appears to you. For some people, the Guardian is male, well-muscled and formidable. For others, a powerful female Guardian appears.

The powerful Guardian protects you and your cottage from entities on the astral plane.

Have no fear of the Guardian. He or she will not hurt you. The Guardian will protect you while you're in the Cottage. When you arrive at the Cottage door, the Guardian will appear. Introduce yourself and tell him or her, "Guardian, this is my Cottage. Thank you for guarding it."

Always acknowledge the Guardian, both when you leave and return. The Guardian will let only you into the Cottage.

About three years ago, I meditated and went onto the astral plane. I went to the door of my Cottage. The Guardian stopped me, and I didn't know why.

Normally I can just walk into my Cottage with no problem, but this time was different.

I felt resistance, almost like I was pressing through a force field. I soon realized that during the resistance the Guardian had stripped off an entity that had latched onto me when I had been on the astral plane. *Thank you, Guardian!* And then I entered my Cottage.

In the following meditation, you will meet your Guardian and then we will proceed to the standing stones or Stone Circle (like those of Stonehenge).

The Stone Circle is another place of protection on the astral plane. This is where you will meet the Gods. In the Stone Circle you can call for or dismiss anything you wish.

You have true power here to affect your environment. Nothing can happen to you that you do not wish to happen. This is one of the "working places" you can go to when you wish to work with the Gods. I suggest always doing your work with the Gods in the Stone Circle.

Meeting the God Ritual

1) Cast the Circle (See Appendix)

2) *Meeting the God Meditation*

Relax. Take a deep breath in. Breathe out, releasing the stresses of the day. Keep taking deep breaths, in and out. With each exhale you get more and more relaxed. Feel your body as it sits comfortably Notice now that the light slowly begins to dim. You feel comfortable and at peace as the light continues to fade. Now the light is gone and you are happy and secure in the darkness.

(Short pause)

Soon you notice the light starts to returns. Slowly at first, it blooms around you. As your eyes adjust to the new light, you see that you are in the Witch's Cottage. The air is fresh and clean. Go to the door leading to the outside and greet the Guardian. The Guardian acknowledges you with a nod, and lets you pass as you step onto the porch. It is a nice clear day, and you smell the plants that grow around the Cottage. You see a path in front of you; it stretches away from the cottage. Walk down the path. Soon you come to a gate at the border of your piece of land that surrounds the Cottage. Go through the gate, and enter a pasture. The path continues for several yards, and you walk it easily.

(Short pause)

You arrive at a fork in the path, graced by a large Oak tree, a lone sentinel on the path before you. At the fork, you see one path to the left and the other to the right. Take the left path and go towards a hill you see in the distance. You find the walk to the hill easy and enjoyable.

(1 minute pause)

Stand at the base of the hill. You see a shape at the top. It is not distinct, but it invites you to come closer. Climb upwards to see what it is.

(Short pause)

You finally reach the top and see a Stone Circle. Now step through the gateway of the Stone Circle.

(Short pause)

As you stand in the middle of the Stone Circle, feel the peace and enjoy the gentle quiet. An occasional bird sings its soothing song on a light gentle breeze. You see a stone altar before you. Kneel before the altar and ask that the God come forth. Relaxed, you wait. Soon a gentle energy forms near you. It's a friendly energy. The God is here. Speak with Him. Listen. Feel His loving presence. Receive His guidance.

(5 minutes pause)

Knowing that your time here with the God is done, you bid Him farewell. Rise to your feet and turn toward the gateway. Pass through the gateway and back onto the path. Walk down the hill and continue on the path to the Cottage.

(Short pause)

The walk is easy and soon you come back to the old Oak Tree.

(Short pause)

Keep walking and arrive at the gate of your piece of land that surrounds the Cottage. Pass through the gate and continue on to the Cottage Door where the Guardian stands, waiting. Greet the Guardian. The Guardian nods in acknowledgment and lets you enter. Now inside the Witch's Cottage, find a nice place and sit. Rest a while. Then notice how the light starts dimming. Feel comfortable and at peace as the light continues to fade. Now the light is gone and you are happy and secure in the darkness.

(Short pause)

Soon you notice that the light starts to return. Slowly at first. Your eyes adjust to the new light and you feel safe, calm and refreshed. Now open your eyes to your present-day world.

3) Do the Cakes and Wine Ceremony (See Appendix)
4) Close the Circle (See Appendix)

* * *

You have now met the God. We can do the same thing to meet the Goddess. We again will travel to the Stone Circle to meet her.

Meet the Goddess Ritual
1) Cast the Circle (See Appendix)
2) Meeting the Goddess Meditation
Relax. Take a deep breath in. Breathe out, releasing the stresses of the day. Keep taking deep breaths, in and out. With each exhale you get more and more relaxed. Feel your body as it sits comfortably Notice now that the light slowly begins to dim. You feel comfortable and at peace as the light continues to fade. Now the light is gone and you are happy and secure in the darkness.

(Short pause)

Soon you notice the light starts to returns. Slowly at first, it blooms around you. As your eyes adjust to the new light, you see that you are in the Witch's Cottage. The air is fresh and clean. Go to the door leading to the outside and greet the Guardian. The Guardian acknowledges you with a nod, and lets you pass as you step onto the porch. It is a nice clear day, and you smell the plants that grow around the Cottage. You see a path in front of you; it stretches away from the cottage. Walk down the path. Soon you come to a gate at the border of your piece of land that surrounds the Cottage. Go through the gate, and enter a pasture. The path continues for several yards, and you walk it easily.

(Short pause)

You arrive at a fork in the path, graced by a large Oak tree, a lone sentinel on the path before you. At the fork, you see one path to the left and the other to the right. Take the left path and go towards a hill you see in the distance. You find the walk to the hill easy and enjoyable.

(1 minute pause)

Stand at the base of the hill. You see the familiar shapes of the Stone Circle. Climb upwards and reach the Stone Circle. Now step through the gateway of the Stone Circle.

(Short pause)

As you stand in the middle of the Stone Circle, feel the peace and enjoy the gentle quiet. An occasional bird sings its soothing song on a light gentle breeze. You see a stone altar before you. Kneel before the altar and ask that the Goddess come forth. Relaxed, you wait. Soon a gentle energy forms near you. It's a friendly energy. The Goddess is here. Speak with Her. Listen. Feel Her loving presence. Receive Her guidance.

(5 minutes pause)

Knowing that your time here with the Goddess is done, you bid Her farewell. Rise to your feet and turn toward the gateway. Pass through the gateway and back onto the path. Walk down the hill and continue on the path to the Cottage.

(Short pause)

The walk is easy and soon you come back to the old Oak Tree.

(Short pause)

Keep walking and arrive at the gate of your piece of land that surrounds the Cottage. Pass through the gate and continue on to the Cottage Door where the Guardian stands, waiting. Greet the Guardian. The Guardian nods in acknowledgment and lets you enter. Now inside the Witch's Cottage, find a nice place and sit. Rest a while. Then notice how the light starts dimming. Feel comfortable and at peace as the light continues to fade. Now the light is gone and you are happy and secure in the darkness.

(Short pause)

Soon you notice that the light starts to return. Slowly at first. Your eyes adjust to the new light and you feel safe, calm and refreshed. Now open your eyes to your present-day world.

3) Do the Cakes and Wine Ceremony (See Appendix)
4) Close the Circle (See Appendix)

Meeting the Gods can be a wonderful experience. I hold my relationships with my Gods close to my heart. I talk with Them everyday and thank them for the blessings in my life.

We've accomplished much with researching specific Gods and Goddesses. You've come to know your Witch's Cottage and one God and one Goddess.

Now, I'll introduce a topic that may be startling to some readers. Your next meditation will include you interacting with a God or Goddess and setting boundaries with the Deity.

Boundaries? Yes. You have a relationship with the Deity and you need to express your personal preferences. Here are some examples of boundaries that Wiccans set with Deities they interact with: a) "no body modification without my approval" and b) "leave my body as you found it." Some Deities are playful and *you* must stress to them what your preferences are.

A number of Wiccan elders have noted that the Gods love us and can be quite enthusiastic about Their involvement in our lives. Sometimes we need to let Them know what is accepted and what isn't. This is where boundaries come in.

Here is a simple way to start the process:

Boundaries Ritual

1) Cast the Circle (See Appendix)
2) *Make Boundaries with Gods (Ritual)*
Relax. Take a deep breath in. Breathe out, releasing the stresses of the day. Keep taking deep breaths, in and out. With each exhale you get more and more relaxed. Feel your body as it sits comfortably Notice now that the light slowly begins to dim. You feel comfortable and at peace as the light continues to fade. Now the light is gone and you are happy and secure in the darkness.

(Short pause)

Soon you notice the light starts to returns. Slowly at first, it blooms around you. As your eyes adjust to the new light, you see that you are in the Witch's Cottage. The air is fresh and clean. Go to the door leading to the outside and greet the Guardian. The Guardian acknowledges you with a nod, and lets you pass as you step onto the porch. It is a nice clear day, and you smell the plants that grow around the Cottage. You see a path in front of you; it stretches away from the cottage. Walk down the path. Soon you come to a gate at the border of your piece of land that surrounds the Cottage. Go through the gate, and enter a pasture. The path continues for several yards and you walk it easily.

(Short pause)

You arrive at a fork in the path, graced by a large Oak tree, a lone sentinel on the path before you. At the fork, you see one path to the left and the other to the right. Take the left path and go towards a hill you see in the distance. You find the walk to the hill easy and enjoyable.

(1 minute pause)

Stand at the base of the hill. You see a shape at the top. It is not distinct, but it invites you to come closer. Climb upwards to see what it is.

(Short pause)

You finally reach the top and see a Stone Circle. Now step through the gateway of the Stone Circle.

(Short pause)

As you stand in the middle of the Stone Circle, feel the peace and enjoy the gentle quiet. An occasional bird sings its soothing song on a light gentle breeze. You see a stone altar before you. Kneel before the altar and ask that the God [or Goddess] come forth. Relaxed, you wait. Soon a gentle energy forms near you. It's a friendly energy. The God [or Goddess] is here. Speak with the Deity. Express what personal boundaries you have and ask the Deity to respect your personal boundaries.

(5 minutes pause)

Knowing that your time here with the God is done, you bid Him farewell. Rise to your feet and turn toward the gateway. Pass through the gateway and back onto the path. Walk down the hill and continue on the path to the Cottage.

(Short pause)

The walk is easy and soon you come back to the old Oak Tree.

(Short pause)

Keep walking and arrive at the gate of your piece of land that surrounds the Cottage. Pass through the gate and continue on to the Cottage Door where the Guardian stands, waiting. Greet the Guardian. The Guardian nods in acknowledgment and lets you enter.

Now inside the Witch's Cottage, find a nice place and sit. Rest a while. Then notice how the light starts dimming. Feel comfortable and at peace as the light continues to fade. Now the light is gone and you are happy and secure in the darkness.

(Short pause)

Soon you notice that the light starts to return. Slowly at first. Your eyes adjust to the new light and you feel safe, calm and refreshed. Now open your eyes to your present-day world.

3) Do the Cakes and Wine Ceremony (See Appendix)
4) Close the Circle (See Appendix)

You can repeat this meditation if you need to make changes or additions to what you express as your personal boundaries.

Just remember to do your research on your Gods and Goddesses, and read multiple sources.

In Perfect Love and In Perfect Trust

During a ritual, Wiccans often express this couplet, "in perfect love and in perfect trust." What does this mean? I have heard many people explain that it is trusting your coven mates, teachers and so forth, perfectly.

Wait a minute! We must be careful. True stories are shared in the Wiccan community about a few unscrupulous people who have used "in perfect love and in perfect trust" as a tool of manipulation.

A manipulator "Henry" says, "Don't you trust me? Remember 'in perfect love and in perfect trust'? I'm telling you that it's right to have sex with me—"

What! Wrong! This guy Henry is a lying manipulator. Do NOT fall for this kind of garbage.

With the above I have clarified that "in perfect love and perfect trust does NOT mean go along with whatever the other person says.

So what does the phrase really mean? "In perfect love and perfect trust" *refers to the Gods*, NOT people.

The phrase is about how the Gods have your best interest at heart. When we realize this, it is easier for us to trust our Gods.

By having perfect trust in your Gods, I do NOT mean having no boundaries. Above we even had a *Making Boundaries with the Gods meditation.*

Healthy boundaries are a must whether in a relationship with a human or a God. You don't want to wake up from a trance and find you have a new tattoo because the Deity you were working with thought it would be a good idea for you.

To continue our theme of being careful, I'll now introduce you to the folly of the Fluffy Bunny.

Beware The Fluffy Bunny!

What is a Fluffy Bunny Pagan?

Patti Wiggington defines a "Fluffy Bunny" in this way: *"In general, 'fluffy bunny,' or 'fluffbunny,' is a derogatory term used to apply to members of the Pagan community who (1) insist that they know everything they need to know, (2) often make blanket statements about what 'real Pagans' do and don't do, and (3) flat-out refuse to acknowledge that people who think differently from them can be Pagan, too."*

If people think they know everything they need to know, they can make serious mistakes. Such arrogance can lead to physical danger. For example, I once read a book that talked about grinding certain stones, putting them in water and drinking the water. **Do NOT do this!** The rocks may contain traces of harmful compounds like arsenic or other poisonous substances.

Further, grinding stones with a high silicon composition is like grinding up glass. Drinking such a solution will turn your insides into hamburger. **Again, don't do it!**

Watch out about herbs, too. Avoid taking the advice of just one book. Check in with an elder or mentor (or two or three). Do NOT experiment on yourself!

Fluffy Bunnies often don't do their research. As a result, they can fall into believing mixed up notions. For example, Wicca is NOT the TV show *Charmed*.

The truth is: Wicca and Paganism have a real history throughout time. It's valuable to study such history and avoid being misguided by something created merely for entertainment. I have heard a number of people say that Fluffy Bunnies have a bad reputation for talking about things in an "everything is butterflies and unicorns" manner.

Fluffy Bunnies, as Patti noted, often make blanket statements about what "real Pagans" do and don't do.

For me, Wicca and Paganism can sometimes appear like herding cats. Everyone has their own ideas of what is the right way. I am Gardnerian, a British tradition. Does that make someone in the Feri tradition wrong? No.

Here's a way to view the situation. Let's say you have a potato. Every tradition cooks the potato differently. One may dice the potato, fry it and enjoy fries. Others mash the potato. Still, others may bake the potato and leave it whole. Does this mean that one is better than the others? No. The people all cooked the potato.

The outcome was the same, just the preparation was

different.

Now, one might say that Fluffy Bunnies are merely cooking the potato in their own way. Fair enough. But if they begin telling you that their way is the 'right' way, then you may want to be wary of them, especially if their ideas appear not to be based in solid research.

How about we aim to be Learned Wiccans or Pagans?

Sounds good to me.

Doing research is just one part of being a Learned Wiccan or Pagan. The other is working with yourself or as I call it, doing inner work, to know yourself.

Now that you have done your research and have done the meditations to meet the Gods and created relationships with them, you may wish to make a *portable shrine*. I love this project because it's fun and you can honor the Gods at the same time. When you are finished you have a nice shrine to keep in your home and the best part is that you can take it with you on vacation!

Have the Gods with You When Travelling: The Portable Shrine

Do you travel a lot? Have you missed viewing your Gods from your home altar? Make a Portable Shrine. It's fun.

What you will need:
- One wooden hinged box (a portable size)
- Different colored tissue paper (I used some paper with a flower-pattern for one of my boxes.)
- Image of the God
- Image of the Goddess
- Glue gun and glue
- Tulip® Dimensional Fabric Paint–Glitter

- Mini-flowers and/or other decorations for the Gods

(For example, I included flowers for the Goddess. You can use beads, paint, coins or other decorations that have meaning for you and your Gods.)

- Electric tea lights. Hotels do **not** let you use lit candles.
- Mod Podge glue
- Sponge applicator (for the Mod Podge glue)
- Other decorations like stickers and such as desired

To start, I used the sponge to apply Mod Podge glue to the exterior surface of my wooden box. Then I affixed the flower-patterned tissue paper to the surface with the glue. Note in the photo how the patterned tissue paper provides an interesting texture. (Be careful to use glue on only one side at a time. If you don't, things will get messy. Also, the glue may dry before you can apply your paper.)

Once I was finished with all sides, then I applied another coat of glue over the tissue paper to seal it.

As another option, you can paint your box any color that seems appropriate, perhaps, your favorite color.

Although you could add decorations to the outside of the box, I suggest leaving it plain. Why? You do not want a hotel maid or other stranger to be drawn to the box out of curiosity.

Inside the box, I used red tissue paper. Pick the color you prefer. Whether you glue paper or paint the inside, be sure to wait for it to dry completely. Then use the glue gun to apply the images of your chosen God and Goddess to the interior of your box.

Note in the photo that I used Tulip® Dimensional Fabric

Paint–Glitter to cover the edges of the Deities' pictures—gold glitter for the God and silver for the Goddess.

I added pearl 3D-stick-ons and other jeweled stick-on pieces to accent my images. I also added glittery stickers on the sides to personalize the interior of my box.

I strung beads in strands—two for the God and one long strand for the Goddess. I used fishing line for that. I draped the beads and used the glue gun to affix the ends in place.

As a finishing touch, I employed the glue gun as I added mini-flowers to the Goddess' side.

Once your Portable Shrine is fully dried, you close it up. From the outside, no one will know what it is.

Take your Portable Shrine anywhere, open it up and place the electric candle in front to honor the God and Goddess.

My Portable Shrine is small and compact enough to fit into a backpack that I bring on a plane. I even took it on a cruise. It's nice to have the familiar company of my shrine when I am away from home.

At home, I place my Portable Shrine in a prominent location and enjoy it.

Since your Portable Shrine is nondescript when closed, it can be placed on a bookshelf or the corner of a desk. Some people consider using a Portable Shrine in a dorm room because the Portable Shrine can be closed quickly.

Making a Portable Shrine can be a fun family project. You could have each family member contribute to one Family Portable Shrine or each person could create his or her own. Perhaps, you might want to do both. They are fun and relatively easy to make.

So keep the craft in witchcraft and have some fun while honoring the Gods.

Along with a portable shrine you might want to consider a House God for your home.

House Gods

When my friend Janet introduced me to her House Goddess, "Phyllis," I was immediately intrigued. How would it feel to have a spiritual being watching over your home and protecting you and your loved ones?

Many cultures focus on House Gods who protect the home in some form. There's Cofgodas in Anglo-Saxon Paganism and Gasin in Korea. Lares, from ancient Rome, protects the home.

Some House Gods just take care of certain rooms. Others oversee certain activities done in a particular room.

My House God's name is Timmy. (I looked at the statue and concentrated and asked, "What is your name?" Immediately, "Timmy" jumped into my thoughts.)

A male House God is unusual in that House Gods tend to be female. Timmy protects my home and my loved ones who reside there. Like a divine watch dog, he keeps mischief at bay. He keeps us safe from negative entities who may wander by.

Many readers may want to invite a House God into their home.

Good news! They're most likely already there.

So how do you entice your House God to take his or her job more seriously?

Make them offerings, of course.

Here is how I began my relationship with Timmy.

I got a statue that I liked. (House Gods tend to take residence in an object.) I found mine at the Northern California Renaissance Pleasure Faire, but you can find your object anywhere.

My statue is also a candle holder, which is a plus for offering candles. And it has the added coolness that the cat eyes glow when you place the candle in the statue.

I placed the statue in a prominent place in my home and then asked that the House God come forward. I invited Timmy to protect my home and all my loved ones who reside in it. And in turn I would honor him by offering him this statue, and I would give him candles with my thanks.

I lit the candle and asked him if this was acceptable. I said, "If you agree, please blink to confirm your answer is 'yes.'" He "blinked" by flickering the fire. That's how our conversation began.

When you start a relationship with your House God, he or she will diligently continue with the protection job. Just make sure to give him or her offerings to say "thank you."

Now let us explore the Witch's Cottage a little more. This next meditation is about the garden that surrounds the cottage. This is a place where you can go to get supplies on the astral plane. You can do magick on the astral plane as well as the physical. The Witch's Cottage is a place to do these type of workings. You can even build relationships with plants and other beings in the garden. Let's explore the garden.

1) Cast the Circle (See Appendix)
2) *The Garden Meditation*
Relax. Take a deep breath in. Breathe out, releasing the stresses of the day. Keep taking deep breaths, in and out. With each exhale you get more and more relaxed. Feel your body as it sits comfortably Notice now that the light slowly begins to dim. You feel comfortable and at peace as the light continues to fade. Now the light is gone and you are happy and secure in the darkness.

(Short pause)

Soon you notice the light starts to return. Slowly at first, it blooms around you. As your eyes adjust to the new light, you see that you are in the Witch's Cottage. The air is fresh and clean. Go to the door leading to the outside and greet the Guardian. The Guardian acknowledges you with a nod and lets you pass as you step onto the porch. It is a nice clear day, and you smell the plants that grow around the Cottage.

Warm and gentle on your face, the sun greets you. Take a few steps and notice a basket sitting on the porch. Pick it up. Glance about your land around the Cottage and see a lovely garden that extends from the Cottage to the gate. The path runs through the middle of the garden, which has an extensive herb garden near your Cottage. The herb plants are in full bloom.

(5 second pause)

Look to your left and see a small orchard that runs along the fence on the boundary of your property.

(5 second pause)

Return your gaze to the center of your property and see the path that runs through the middle of your garden Step off the porch and walk the path through your garden. Admire the sights and smells of all the new growth and life that abound in the garden. Step off the path and pick up a few of the treasures of your garden and place them into your basket. Glance about your garden. Perhaps, there are a couple of neighborly animals. Maybe a squirrel or a friendly rabbit. Hear a song of a bird that passes overhead.

(5 minutes pause)

Breathe in deeply the fragrant air. Now done with your garden you turn toward your Cottage. Step on the path and return to your porch. Greet the Guardian, who nods and lets you pass. Enter your Witch's Cottage and place the basket on a small table next to the fireplace.
Take some of your treasures that you found in the garden and place them on the hearth above your warm, crackling fireplace. Select an item or two to offer to the Gods. Hold an item in your hand and say, "I honor you, Lord and Lady and thank you for the abundance of my garden."

(5 minutes pause)

Rest a while. Then notice how the light starts dimming. Feel comfortable and at peace as the light continues to fade. Now the light is gone and you are happy and secure in the darkness.

(Short pause)

Soon you notice that the light starts to return. Slowly at first. Your eyes adjust to the new light and you feel safe, calm and refreshed. Now open your eyes to your present-day world.

3) Do the Cakes and Wine Ceremony (See Appendix)
4) Close the Circle (See Appendix)

You can return to your Witch's Cottage whenever you

want and continue to decorate it and the surrounding area.

Now, we'll return to the oak tree. The following mediation gives you an experience of the cycle of life and renewal of the spirit.

Old Oak Tree Mediation Ritual

1) Cast the Circle (See Appendix)

2) *Meeting the Mighty Oak meditation*

Relax. Take a deep breath in. Breathe out, releasing the stresses of the day. Keep taking deep breaths, in and out. With each exhale you get more and more relaxed. Feel your body as it sits comfortably Notice now that the light slowly begins to dim. You feel comfortable and at peace as the light continues to fade. Now the light is gone and you are happy and secure in the darkness.

(Short pause)

Soon you notice the light starts to return. Slowly at first, it blooms around you. As your eyes adjust to the new light, you see that you are in the Witch's Cottage. The air is fresh and clean. Go to the door leading to the outside and greet the Guardian. The Guardian acknowledges you with a nod and lets you pass as you step onto the porch. It is a nice clear day and you step off the porch to the path the runs through your garden. Enjoy the sweet smells of the herbs and fruit-bearing trees. See your gate at the edge of the garden and walk to the gate. Pass through the gate, and enter the pasture. You walk easily on the path until you come to the large oak tree at the fork in the path. Look at the magnificent wise old tree. Then walk to your right and stop when you're on the opposite side of the tree.

Find a small opening in the trunk of the tree. Crouch a little and comfortably go into the tree. Feel peace and love surround you. Stand in the cozy hollow within the old tree. Gently sit down. Relax. Your consciousness sinks down and you feel your consciousness mix with the roots—you feel the nourishing earth that surrounds the roots. You feel the energy from the earth, filling you. More than that, you feel one with Mother Earth.

(5 seconds pause)

Feel Mother Earth's life force; you are part of Earth's nourishing life force.

(5 seconds pause)

Flow into the roots and up into the trunk. You're drawn into the branches. You feel one with the branches. Then you focus on one branch, then the tip of that branch. You feel one with the bud that starts to bloom. Now as that bud you become a new leaf. As the leaf, feel and enjoy the sun's rays shining on you, warming you up. Feel yourself fill with strength.

(5 seconds pause)

Now you are a mature and strong leaf. As this leaf you experience the sun, the moon, the rain, the wind, the day and night. Experience the full beauty and life as a leaf on this tree.

(3 minutes pause)

Now, having experienced a full life as a leaf, begin to wither with age. You feel calm. You are not afraid of death because you know that you will simply return to Mother Earth to be reborn.

(5 seconds pause)

With a gentle kiss from a slight breeze, as the leaf, you let go and separate from the old oak tree. Slowly and blissfully, you float down and gently land on the Earth. During this restful time, you remember your life as a leaf. Mother Earth takes you back within her.

(5 seconds pause)

You dissolve and become one with the soil. You become one with Mother Earth's nourishing life force. Notice your familiar root in the earth. Enter and move up the root to the heart of the old oak tree. You arrive back in your own body sitting in the hollow of the old oak tree. You feel refreshed and renewed. Sit for a time, feeling comfortable in the hollow of this tree. Then rise to your feet and emerge from the tree. Walk back to the front of the old tree. Thank the tree for its wisdom. Take leave of this great sentinel and go back the way you came. Walk through the pasture. The path continues for several yards and you walk easily.

(Short Pause)

Keep walking and arrive at the gate of your piece of land that surrounds the Cottage. Pass through the gate and continue on to the Cottage Door where the

Guardian stands, waiting. Greet the Guardian. The Guardian nods in acknowledgment and lets you enter. Now inside the Witch's Cottage, find a nice place and sit. Rest a while. Then notice how the light starts dimming. Feel comfortable and at peace as the light continues to fade. Now the light is gone and you are happy and secure in the darkness.

(Short pause)

Soon you notice that the light starts to return. Slowly at first. Your eyes adjust to the new light and you feel safe, calm and refreshed. Now open your eyes to your present-day world.

3) Do the Cakes and Wine Ceremony (See Appendix)
4) Close the Circle (See Appendix)

Now that you have experienced the above meditations, you know the basic building blocks to create your own meditations. Modify the ones you experienced or start fresh and make your own. Still, continue to use the structure of Cast the Circle, Conduct the Meditation, Do the Cakes and Wine Ceremony and Close the Circle.

In the next chapter, we explore rituals that emphasize the cycles of the seasons.

CHAPTER 5:
RITUALS TO BRING US CLOSER TO THE GODS AND TO ALIGN WITH THE CYCLES OF THE SEASONS (AND SELECT SPELLS)

Wiccans celebrate the Sabbats as a great way to attune oneself to the changes of the seasons and align with the rhythms of Mother Earth. In this chapter, we'll explore some simple Sabbat celebrations followed by Esbat rites.

What are Sabbats and Esbats? A Sabbat is one of the eight major festival/celebrations in the Wiccan calendar.

Let's begin with a discussion about rituals.

Why Do Wiccans Do Ritual?

Wiccans do ritual to feel the presence of the Gods and Goddesses.

It was a tough time. Bills were closing in on me. I felt desperate. I reached for something that is constant: The presence of the Gods and Goddesses. How did I feel Their presence? I did a ritual.

Furthermore, Wiccans do rituals to attune themselves to

Moonwater SilverClaw

the cycles of the earth.

Sometimes we do ritual to change ourselves for the better. We even change how we perceive ourselves, and in so doing, change the world around us.

Because of all of the above, ritual is a powerful tool.

We use some rituals to acknowledge the different stages of life, and in this way change ourselves forever. Stages include: reaching puberty, graduation, hand-fasting (Wiccan Marriage), giving birth, and even for reaching Elder status.

Ritual can help us create a true understanding of ourselves. We take a first step to a new reality for us. We get a new perception that assists us to make different decisions which can completely change our lives.

Above, I talked about the tough time with bills closing in. That was 2012. I needed to change my reality. So I did a ritual. In preparation for that ritual, I used another tool— meditation.

The meditation (which can be a ritual in and of itself) led me to the answer of doing a particular ritual.

Enduring financial troubles, I needed more income. I had tried the quick-fix spells for more money. Those spells backfired. So if these spells were not working, what would?

I needed to do some *inner change*. So I did a ritual in which I asked to become stronger, to be able to create my own abundance in life. This is what I needed. *Not* another spell to just dump money in my lap. But to be able to be my own catalyst in my own life. This was inner work; this was changing *me*—not just temporarily altering an external situation.

A short time after completing my ritual, I had a vision from the Gods: I was to write my first book, *The Hidden Children of the Goddess*.

By doing the ritual, I was the catalyst in my own life. I

had never written an article. But I had received a vision from the Gods, so I began to write. Because I have dyslexia, I engaged a team of editors. While writing the book, I started writing my blog which now has viewers in over 138 countries.

By meditating, then doing a ritual and then receiving a vision from the Gods, I was on a new path as a writer. In becoming a writer, I then became a workshop leader.

So I am living proof that doing a ritual can change your life. And it can start a positive cascade effect until you uplift those around you. And some of us go further so that a ritual is the start of our changing the world.

So now it's your turn. Change your world! Make new possibilities bloom in your life and in the lives of others. Listen to your heart. What would you like a ritual to do for you? Look at resources like my book *The Hidden Children of the Goddess* for rituals and meditations you can do.

Remember the Gods are always with you. Do a ritual and feel Their support.

* * *

The Down and Dirty about Love Spells

"I really like this guy. Can you do a love spell for me?" Wiccans are faced with this question a lot.

Love spells can be quite sticky. There's a right way and a wrong way to approach them.

The Wrong Way to Do a Love Spell

Janet really likes Mark. So she buys a book on love spells from the local book store. She finds one she likes and performs the spell that night on Mark.

The next day she sees Mark. There's something different

about him. Soon he asks Janet for a date. During the date Mark can't keep his eyes off Janet.

In the next days, Mark can't get enough of Janet. At first she quite enjoys the attention. He calls every night.

Then he follows her to the gym, grocery store, a movie theater. He shows up at her house unexpectedly, at all hours of the day and night.

Now, every time she sees Mark, Janet jumps, startled.

Janet wanted love; she now has fear.

Do you see what happened? Janet made her own stalker by casting a love spell upon him. Two terrible details arise when you impose a love spell on someone. First, it's unethical to tamper with someone's free will. Second, you could create a pattern in which a stalker may become violent.

The Right Way to Cast a Love Spell

Ellen hasn't been on a date in quite a while. At an evening class she attends each week, she likes three guys, but she's not sure about them.

She wants to find the right fit and someone who truly loves her. So Ellen decides to do a love spell. Ellen first decides to make the love spell about herself—that is, she seeks to become more accepting of love. During her ritual, she writes down what she'd prefer to find in a mate. She asks the Gods to guide her and that special person to meet.

A few days later, a guy named Sam arrives at the evening class. Sam is meeting one of the other three guys who attend the evening class. Sam strikes up a conversation with Ellen. Some days later, Sam asks Ellen out on a date. They really hit it off.

Do you see the difference?

Janet did a love spell on Mark, and such an imposition should never be done.

On the other hand, Ellen did a love spell to make *herself* more accepting of love and to be able to see the one she was looking for. She also asked the Gods to help guide both her and her right match to find each other.

That's a big difference.

Love Spell

What you will need:

- Pink candle (a small one that can be burned in one hour)
- Rose Oil to dress the candle. (You can make Rose Oil by diluting rose essential oil into olive oil. Make sure it is the therapeutic grade essential oil.)
- Candle holder for pink candle
- Lodestone
- Table for the altar
- Candles and candleholders for the four directions in the colors that represent each (red for south, blue for west, green for north, yellow for east)
- Red candle for the God and a green candle for the Goddess. (These candle colors are preferable but not mandatory. You may also use white candles, which represent all colors.)
- Working candle to represent the element Fire
- Cup or chalice
- Athame
- Pentagram
- Sword (If you don't have one, use an athame to cast the circle.)
- Incense

- Censer
- Dish of salt, preferably sea salt
- Bowl of water
- Bell or chime
- Altar cloth to keep wax and the other things off the table
- Wine or juice and some sort of cake
- Lighter
- Taper (Light the taper by using the working candle. Then use the taper to light the other candles.)

1) Cast the Circle (See Appendix)

2) *The Love Spell*

Take up the pink candle and sprinkle some of the blessed water on it and say:

You are cleansed by water and earth.

Next wave the pink candle over the burning incense and say:

I charge and consecrate you by fire and air.

Do the same process with the rose oil and the lodestone.

Next take your now cleansed and consecrated pink candle and carve your name on it with the word love.

Next dress the candle with the rose oil and say:

Little candle, I name you (your name). You now represent the love I attract to me.

Place the pink candle into the candle holder and place on the pentagram. Put the lodestone at the base of the candle.

Take the taper and light it from the working candle and light the pink candle saying:

I am love and love comes to me.

As the candle burns sit and concentrate on the candle flame, seeing love flowing in the form of light. When the candle has burned halfway down, take the candle and drop three drops of wax on the lodestone. Return the candle to its original place.

Continue to see the love radiating from the candle, and now also see the lodestone pulling love to you.

Watch the candle until it burns completely out. Carry the stone with you to help attract love to you.

3) Do the Cakes and Wine Ceremony (See Appendix)
4) Close the Circle (See Appendix)

In the section before the proper Love Spell, I advised you to avoid the wrong way to do a love spell.

Take care in how you go about doing a proper Love Spell, which will build you up and attract the right match for you.

[If you're interested in prosperity spells and other spells, please see my book *The Hidden Children of the Goddess* and *Beyond the Law of Attraction to Real Magic: How You Can Remove Blocks to Prosperity, Happiness and Inner Peace.*]

After our discussion of certain spells, we'll now explore Sabbat Rituals.

Sabbat Rituals

The following are rituals, or Sabbats, for the turning of the Wheel of the Year which is the Wiccan calendar that honors the cycles of the year.

Wiccans view the Wiccan calendar as a wheel because it has no beginning and no end. The wheel continuously turns from one season to the next.

You'll notice the Sabbats illustrate the cycle of life and the cycle of the seasons. You'll see how these simple rituals may be fun for you, your coven, and/or your family. For each Sabbat I will give a brief explanation of what is happening during the time of the rite.

Samhain Ritual

The final harvest Sabbat, Samhain, celebrates the period of the year when the last crops are gathered and put into storage for the cold winter months. Samhain arrives at the time that the Western World calls Halloween.

At this Sabbat, the God makes his ultimate sacrifice. But fear not! His sacrifice is made willingly. He does it for his children. The God's sacrifice is represented by the final harvest being cut down so that we may have food to last through the winter. The song, "John Barleycorn," illustrates this sacrifice well. This Sabbat is also the Witches New Year which is why I've placed it first.

What you will need:
- Fire proof container
- Sand (to put into container) for the incense
- Dragon's blood stick incense
- Lighter or matches
- Bell
- Lots of tea light candles
- Veil to cover ancestor altar until it is "opened"
- Cakes and wine
- Music with wolf howling for playback
- A song (for example, "Funeral for a Friend" by Elton John) for playback
- Another song (for example, "Into the West" as featured in the closing credits of the feature film, *The Lord of the Rings: The Return of the King.*)
- A music player
- Anything that has belonged to a deceased loved one or photos of deceased loved ones*

* Set up a small altar, the "ancestor altar" to the West (in the western area of the room you're holding the ritual in). Place photos of deceased loved ones on this altar and place a veil over them.

Samhain Rite

Before you begin, you will need:

- A table for the altar.
- Candles and candleholders for the four directions in the colors that represent each (red for south, blue for west, green for north, and yellow for east)
- A red candle for the God and a green candle for the Goddess. These candle colors are preferable but not mandatory. You may also use white candles, which represent all colors.
- A working candle to represent the element Fire.
- A cup or chalice.
- An athame.
- A sword. If you don't have one, use the athame to cast the circle.
- Incense and incense burner.
- A dish of salt, preferably sea salt.
- A bowl of water.
- A bell or chime.
- An altar cloth to keep wax and the other things off the table.
- Wine or juice
- Some sort of cake.
- A lighter.
- A taper (to light the other candles from the working candle).

1) Cast the Circle (See Appendix)

2) *Samhain Rite*

Playback the music with wolf howling so that it plays in the background throughout this rite.

High Priestess says:

We are here to rejoice with our ancestors once more. We shall now pull back the veil and shall name our beloved dead and ask that they join us in this circle tonight.

High Priestess and High Priest each take a corner of the veil and lift it from altar of the dead that is in the West, as all chant:

We pull back the veil

(Ring Bell)

We pull back the veil

(Ring Bell)

We pull back the veil

(Ring Bell)

High Priestess says:

The veil is now open! Let us call upon our beloved dead and call our ancestors.

One by one members come up and take a stick of incense and light it, using the working candle. Then each person takes a tea light candle (representing one of their ancestors) and lights the tea light candle.

Example:

Person (lighting incense) places it on the altar: **To all of my Ancestors**

All Reply: **To [Person's Ancestors] we honor you!**

(Ring Bell)

Person (lighting tea light candle): **[Name of dead person]**

All Reply: **[Name of dead person] we honor you!**
(Ring Bell)

Members then place each tea light candle on the altar in turn. Once all have finished naming their beloved,

High Priest says:
Beloved dead we are honored with your presence.

High Priestess says: **Thank you for joining with us on this special night, O beloved dead. Let us dance in your honor.**

High Priestess presses the button on a music player and all hear the song (for example, "Funeral for a Friend" by Elton John).

All dance in a circle.
All reminisce and tell stories of their deceased loved ones.
Upon completion:

High Priest: says:
Beloved Dead we thank you for joining us in circle and now you must go back to the land from whence you came.

High Priestess plays another song on the music player (for example, "Into the West" as featured in the closing credits of the feature film, *The Lord of the Rings: The Return of the King*.)

High Priest and High Priestess place veil back onto the altar of the dead that is in the West as all chant:
We place back the veil

(Ring Bell)
We place back the veil
(Ring Bell)
We place back the veil
(Ring Bell)

High Priestess says:
The veil between the worlds is once more closed.

3) Do the Cakes and Wine Ceremony (See Appendix)
4) Close the Circle (See Appendix)

* * * * * *

Yule Ritual

Yule is also known as the Winter Solstice, the longest night of the year. During early human history, people feared that the sun would not reappear without help. With this belief began the custom of lighting candles and fires to lure back the sun. It was believed that this ritual would help the God to be reborn (as the Solar Deity) from the Goddess. The ritual would help the Goddess have an easy delivery.

At some time before Yule and when we do this ritual, the Goddess has transformed back into her youthful form, as the young virgin mother.

At Yule the Goddess is pregnant with the God.

For this ritual, get a Yule log and make sure to have three indentations on the Yule log. We will place a candle in each indentation.

Yule Rite

What you will need:
- Rattle
- Yule log
- Three candles (one of each of these colors: green, red and white. Each candle must fit the indentation on the Yule log)
- Veil (to cover the Yule log)
- Beverage
- A glass for each person
- An offering to the newborn God (something small, preferably biodegradable, such as a piece of fruit)

1) Cast the Circle (See Appendix)
2) *Yule Rite*
High Priest says:
The Wheel again turns around to the beginning that has no beginning. Ever turning ever renewing. And as the wheel turns the Goddess prepares herself for the great event. The Goddess calls out the names of her lover son. Bidding his arrival.

High Priest shakes the rattle.

Coven Members chant the names of the God:
Pan, Cernunnos, Zeus, Apollo, Helios, Osiris, Mithras

High Priestess and High Priest each grab a corner of the veil and lift the veil off the Yule log, as the chanting continues.

High Priestess rings the bell.

High Priest says:
The Goddess can now feel the universe as it churns inside her swollen belly.

High Priestess lights the green candle.

Coven Members continue chanting:
Pan, Cernunnos, Zeus, Apollo, Helios, Osiris, Mithras

High Priestess rings bell.

High Priest says:
The God is coming!

High Priestess lights the red candle.

Coven Members continue chanting:
Pan, Cernunnos, Zeus, Apollo, Helios, Osiris, Mithras

High Priestess rings the bell quite loudly. And the Coven Members stop chanting.

High Priest says:
The God is here!

High Priestess lights the white candle.

High Priestess says:
We toast you, God and Goddess.

All raise their glasses.

Make offerings to the newborn God.

(Each person puts his or her offering on the altar. Each person says something like: "Thank you" or "We welcome you, God.")

If desired, gifts can be exchanged among the Coven Members at this moment.

3) Do the Cakes and Wine Ceremony (See Appendix)
4) Close the Circle (See Appendix)

You've now learned of the Yule Ritual. Unfortunately, many Wiccans don't feel the love and joy at this time of year. So how do you overcome the Yuletide blues?

Overcoming Yuletide Blues

Are you less than jolly this time of year? Tired of hearing how happy you're supposed to be during the holidays? Do you just want more peace during this stressful time?

Some of us find it a hardship to see relatives who don't share our spiritual beliefs.

Many Wiccans and Pagans stay in the broom closet (in hiding) from family and friends. Why? Rejection. Some families even banish Pagan relatives. This banishment would result if they discovered our hearts and minds are with the Gods. It's just too much of a risk of loss for many to bear. In some communities, one may even fear retaliation by one's own family.

I know some Pagans who don't face such consequences and who practice freely. These fortunate Pagans told me that the others are "cowards" for hiding. It bothers me to witness such lack of compassion for others' pain and problems.

How do we cope with such adversity?

Being in the broom closet is not necessarily a bad thing. For some, it is a necessity for keeping their job and family.

So how do we keep the peace in our own hearts this holiday season while in the closet? How do we still honor the Gods during the holidays with family? Here are a few suggestions:

- Wear a pagan pendant under your shirt. (Just make sure that it can't fall out and be seen by unfriendly eyes.)
- Light a candle (while saying a silent prayer) and place it on the mantel or other place of prominence in your own home.
- Take a ritual bath before a gathering and honor the Gods. You'll feel better.
- Bring a bottle of your favorite drink (mead is mine) to a gathering.
- Anoint yourself with sacred oil and keep your intentions of love and peace for the Yule holiday close to you.

These actions can be done in the broom closet and need not require permission from any unsympathetic family members.

And for that extra touch of magick here is a simple blessing you can say for yourself for holiday gatherings.

By the Gods and the four quarters' might,
May this blessing be just right.
May the Gods love be in my heart,
May my heart be the center for my kindness,
May my kindness be a guide for my compassion,
May my compassion be an action of love in this world,
And may my action of love in this world bring peace to

all at this time.
So mote it be.

* * *

For some of us, Yule brings painful feelings and even grief. Have you experienced loss at this time of year? I have, and here are a few words on loss at Yule time.

Death and Grief during Yule Time

A dear friend of mine was shot and killed at his workplace [in December 2013]. While I'm writing section of this book, I'm grieving and I'm angry because I feel his death could have been prevented.

Grieving during the holidays when everyone is supposed to be so cheerful feels especially painful. In our pain, we might even feel anger take hold. It's unfair to be singled out for grief.

So what can you do for a person in grief? Just listen to her.

Listening to a person dealing with grief is a hard thing. It often brings up our own pain.

Listening is a gift you give to help the grieving person feel needed support. Saying what she feels can even begin her healing process.

It's true that you can't solve anything for the person. But you don't need to, and you shouldn't try. The person grieving must travel the path of healing herself.

Being there for your friend or family member is the best thing you can do. Offering a kind heart, an understanding shoulder and an attentive ear is the best gift you can give someone going through grief.

May all those who cross to the other side this Yule Time be blessed, and may those who are left behind be blessed as well. So mote it be.

* * * * * *

The Wheel of the Year now turns towards Imbolc.

Imbolc Ritual

Midway between the Winter Solstice and the Spring Equinox, you will find Imbolc, which is celebrated on February 2nd. This time of year the light is beginning to return to the world. Like the Yule Sabbat, the Imbolc Sabbat is also associated with fire. Imbolc is a time of purification. A popular rite is jumping over a blessed fire. This next ritual echoes these themes.

* * *

Imbolc Rite

What you will need:
- Cauldron (to hold a white candle)
- White Candle

1) Cast the Circle (See Appendix)
2) *Imbolc Rite*
Place cauldron in the middle of circle on the floor. Place white candle inside the cauldron.

High Priestess says:
Today is the point of mid winter. We now call upon Bridget's light to guide us through to spring and purify our homes and ourselves.

High Priestess lights candle in the caldron and says:
With this candle with Bridget's light may we all be blessed and purified.

All dance around the cauldron while chanting:
Winter, winter go away,
We've had enough of you this day.
Winter, winter go away,
With purity for all to stay.
Winter, winter go away,
Bring us summer's warmth soon to stay.

Each dancer jumps over the cauldron in turn so that they can be blessed and purified. (*Be careful* not to bump the cauldron.)

After the last person jumps over the cauldron, the singers all raise their hands up and exclaim:
So mote it be!

3) Do the Cakes and Wine Ceremony (See Appendix)
4) Close the Circle (See Appendix)

* * * * * *

Ostara Ritual

Ostara takes place at the Spring (Vernal) Equinox. The length of the day becomes equal to that of the night, and the light finally overcomes the darkness of winter. Ostara's theme is fertility. The God courts the Goddess, and their sexual energies of desire flow over the Earth. This leads to a burst of new life and growth upon the land by the plants and the animals. Here the God and Goddess's desire to mate drives the Earth and its inhabitants to also mate and bring new life to the land. Wiccans celebrate Ostara to help bring this fertility to the world and into our own lives.

* * *

Ostara Rite

What you will need:
- Large hollow chocolate rabbit
- Basket
- Easter basket grass
- Jelly beans
- Toy bird
- Veil to cover chocolate rabbit

Preparation: Take hollow chocolate rabbit and make a small hole in the bottom. Fill chocolate rabbit with jelly beans. Place rabbit in a basket with Easter grass (be careful not to spill the jelly beans from the rabbit). Place basket onto the middle of the altar.

1) Cast the Circle (See Appendix)
2) *Ostara Rite*
High Priestess tells the story:
Ostara, the Goddess of Spring, once came across a bird with a broken wing. The bird shivers, cold and dying from its injury. Ostara, with compassion in her heart, picked up the bird and cradled it in her arms, healing the bird.

Yet the bird could no longer fly. So Ostara turned it into a rabbit.

High Priestess reveals the chocolate rabbit in the basket .

And she gave the rabbit the ability to lay eggs.

High Priestess lifts chocolate rabbit slightly and a couple of jelly bean eggs fall from its bottom.

High Priestess says:
On the Spring equinox each year, the rabbit lays eggs and gives them to others to bless them with fertility. Such fertility may be physical or an increase in prosperity — for the Spring and the coming year.

High Priestess passes the basket of both chocolate rabbit and jelly beans around. Each person partakes of a few "eggs" (jelly beans).

High Priestess asks:
What do you wish to be fertile in this year?

Each person responds with what he or she wants to be fertile in.

High Priestess says:
We now sacrifice this blessed [chocolate] rabbit to honor the beautiful and gracious goddess Ostara.

High Priest breaks the chocolate rabbit into pieces to share. Participants then pass around the basket and each takes a piece of chocolate.

High Priestess says:
May you be blessed.

All eat a piece of chocolate.

3) Do the Cakes and Wine Ceremony (See Appendix)
4) Close the Circle (See Appendix)

* * * * * *

Beltane Ritual

The Sabbat Beltane coincides with the period of time when the God actually impregnates the Goddess. This sacred act insures the continued fertility for crops and animals throughout the time of the year when the Sun is more prominent (between the Spring and Fall Equinoxes.) A popular symbol for this sacred act is the May Pole, which represents the impregnation of the Goddess.

The May Pole stands tall when set in the ground and its ribbons, attached on the top, flutter in the wind. People then each take a ribbon and dance in a weaving pattern around the pole. The pole represents the God's phallus, and the colorful ribbons that the dancers wind around the May Pole represent the Goddess. And so the impregnation of the Goddess is fulfilled.

Wiccans often set up a bonfire at Beltane. Fire represents fertility at this time. Jumping the Beltane bonfire is a well-known fertility activity for this Sabbat.

You don't have to be asking for fertility of the womb to take advantage of the energies of this Sabbat. You can also can ask for fertility for certain situations in your life. However, Wiccans most often focus on fertility in this Sabbat for the land and the animals.

What you will need:
- Cauldron
- Candle(s) preferably three
- Crown of flowers

- Crown of ivy or horned helm
- Pine-cone-tipped wand (standing for the phallic wand)
- Ribbons (9 inches long)
- Noisemakers like rattles and drums

1) Cast the Circle (See Appendix)

2) *Beltane Ritual*

Usually the High Priest and High Priestess portray the God and Goddess respectively. Usually a mated couple play the roles. The role of the God, also known as the May King must be a fertile and mature male. The Goddess, also know as the May Queen, wears a crown of flowers.

The May King dons a crown of ivy.

Each person of the coven is given a ribbon.

High Priest says:

Think of how you wish fertility to come into your life this year.

Setting up the space, a member of the coven places the cauldron in the middle of the circle space. He or she also place candle(s) inside.

(If you don't have a cauldron you can use a bowl and some tea lights. On the other hand, if you have a fire pit, it's better to use actual fire.)

High Priestess says:

I am the fertile maid, and I am awaiting for my love.

High Priest says:

I am the virile God, and I am here to woo my love.

The High Priestess (May Queen) lights the candles and says:

As the wheel turns to the light half of the year, so I light the fire of fertility of the year. As the light grows so do the fertile energies.

(Coven Members shake rattles and beat drums continually through the rest of the ritual.)

The High Priest (May King) takes the pine-cone wand and gestures around the circle and says:

As the wheel turns, the lights grows, so fertility comes to the lands around us.

High Priest points the pine-cone wand at the High Priestess and says:

My lady, I woo thee, accept my advances now, my love!

High Priest (representing the God) then playfully chases the High Priestess (representing the Goddess) as she plays hard to get. During this fun pantomime, the High Priestess beckons the High Priest on. The noises of the rattles and drums speed up in tempo and the chase continues till the God catches the Goddess in a loving embrace and kisses her. (The music comes to a temporary stop)

High Priestess and High Priestess say together:
Now we are one and fertility comes to all and the land!

(Coven Members again shake rattles and beat drums slowly at first and then with increasing intensity.)

High Priest then passes the pine-cone wand to the first Coven Member (a female) and says:
This representation of our fertility, now is your fertility.

The female coven member ties her ribbon to the end of the

wand and says:

As the land's fertility grows, so does my [the object she wants to grow]'s fertility grow!

The female coven member then hands the pine-cone wand to a male coven member and says:

This is the representation of the God's fertility and now is your fertility!

Then the female coven member starts to dance around the cauldron.

The male covener ties his ribbon to the end of the wand and says:

As the land's fertility grows, so does my [the object she wants to grow]'s fertility grow!

This process continues as male coven member then passes the pine-cone wand to a female coven member until all have completed the steps.

The last coven member hands the pine-cone wand back to the High Priest.

All dance to the beating of the drums and rattles and jump over the candles to insure fertility, until the final crescendo and then they all say:

So mote it be!

3) Do the Cakes and Wine Ceremony (See Appendix)
4) Close the Circle (See Appendix)

* * * * * *

Litha Ritual

Litha, also known as both the Summer Solstice and Midsummer, represents when the God is at the height of his power and fertility. The sun now takes its longest path across the sky, and we experience the longest day of the year. This completes the sun's waxing cycle and marks the beginning of the waning part of the solar year. The days become increasingly shorter until the Wheel of the Year returns to Yule when the days once again wax with the sun.

What you will need:

- Sunflower Cupcakes for cakes and wine (You can order cupcakes at your local bakery and specify that you want designs of sunflowers on them.)
- Phallic Candle (You can purchase one or carve a candle in the appropriate shape.)
- Hotdogs/Sausages and other barbeque-ables.
- Music of choice for summer
- Barbeque grill

Remember when you cast circle, make sure to cast a large enough space. For example, you will be including the barbeque grill and circle of chairs.

* * * * * *

Litha Rite

1) Cast the Circle (See Appendix)

2) *Litha Rite*

Place food to be barbequed on the altar along with the cupcakes and candle. Set half of the Sunflower Cupcakes around the Phallic Candle.

All Coven Members assemble around the altar.

High Priest says:

It is summer and this is my time. Revel in the bounty before you. Sing, laugh, kiss, feast and dance, all in my

honor.

High Priestess leads a spiral dance* around the altar.
(* *You may wish to look up the details of a spiral dance online.*)
All focus their energy to the food as they dance. At the end of the dance, High Priest lights the Phallic candle and says:
My fertility spreads across the lands. May all be blessed by it.

Special Cakes and Wine Ceremony: After the cakes and wine have been blessed, everyone grabs a cupcake and takes a turn and talks about what they are looking forward to manifesting this summer. Then each Coven Member takes a bite out of his or her cupcake and the others say:
So mote it be!

When all have finished, High Priestess and High Priest takes the rest of the food and Phallic Candle outside (if not already there) and the barbeque grill is lit using the Phallic Candle's flame.

High Priest says:
Fire, fire burning bright, in the forest, warm and bright. Burning, churning flames alight, sacred fire bless this site.

High Priestess and High Priest bless the food that will be placed on the (sacred) barbeque grill.
At this point you can close the circle and then invite friends and family over for a barbeque gathering.

3) Close the Circle (See Appendix)

This ritual is a great way to include friends and family into your celebration. You can also do other activities like playing a Piñata game (choose a Piñata shaped like the sun). Be creative. The point is to have fun and make it a great gathering.

* * * * * *

Lammas Ritual

On August 1st, Lammas, starts the first of the three Wiccan harvest festivals. Lammas, also known as Lughnasadh occurs on the Celtic first day of autumn. Known as the time when the God starts to wane in his power, Lammas, or "loaf-mass," celebrates the first grains harvested that season. During the Lammas Sabbat, Wiccans offer up the first sheaf of the harvest to the God and Goddess to thank them for their blessing of the harvest yield.

What you will need:
- Loaf of bread that is shaped in a human form (you make your own and you may use a gingerbread man pan)
- Song "John Barleycorn Must Die"

* * *

Lammas Rite

1) Cast the Circle (See Appendix)
2) *Lammas Rite*
High Priest holds the loaf of bread up and says:
Here me now, for I am John Barleycorn, the God of the

grain. Here is my body whole and pure.

High Priest then sets the loaf on the altar that rests in the middle of the circle. High Priest plays the recording of the song "John Barleycorn Must Die." All Coven Members take up hands and dance around the loaf (which stands in for John Barleycorn).

When the song is finished, all bow to the loaf, John Barleycorn.

The Coven Members pass the loaf around the circle with each person giving thanks to John Barleycorn for his sacrifice.

The High Priestess then takes the boline and cuts the loaf in the symbolic manner of cutting John Barleycorn's head off.

All chant:

Marry Meet, Merry Part, and Merry Meet again.

The High Priestess holds up the loaf-head and says:

We offer up John Barleycorn and give thanks for the food he provides his children. To the Gods!

All reply:

To the Gods!

The Coven Members each take a piece of the loaf and consume it.

3) Do the Cakes and Wine Ceremony (See Appendix)
4) Close the Circle (See Appendix)

* * * * * *

Mabon Ritual

Mabon, known as the Autumn Equinox, is the time when day and night are the same length. After Mabon occurs, the days grow shorter. With longer nights and fewer daylight hours, we observe the continued waning power of the God.

What you will need:
- Red candle
- Green candle
- White candle
- Brown candle
- Slips of paper
- Cauldron for burning the slips of paper
- Pens (before the ritual begins be sure to bless these pens—See Appendix)

Note: You may want to do this ritual outside due to the smoke of the burning papers.

1) Cast the Circle (See Appendix)
2) *Mabon Rite*
High Priestess ritually cleanses the Red and Green candles and consecrates them.

The High Priestess takes the Green candle and the High Priest takes the Red candle.

The High Priest holds up the Red candle and says:
I am the light half of the year.

High Priestess holds up the Green candle and says:
I am the dark half of the year.

High Priest and High Priestess say together:
As the year is in balance with the light and the dark of

the year today, we honor the transition from light to dark here and now.

High Priest lights the red candle on the working candle and then says:

I, the light half of the year, now kneel to the dark half of the year.

High Priest lights High Priestess's Green candle with the flame of the Red candle.

High Priestess says:

And so the wheel turns.

Next each Coven Member takes a slip of paper and writes on it something that he or she is thankful for. The person then sets the slip of paper alight, using the Brown candle. The person places the burning paper into the cauldron. He or she says:

So mote it be.

3) Do the Cakes and Wine Ceremony (See Appendix)
4) Close the Circle (See Appendix)

* * *

In this chapter, we have explored the different rituals of The Wheel of the Year. Wiccans find it comforting and enriching to consistently do ritual throughout the year.

CHAPTER 6:
THE ESBATS

Wiccans focus on The Esbats as times when we honor the God and the Goddess on the full of the moon. Wiccan often tie the ritual to the season. An Esbat is a Wiccan meeting at the time of the full moon.

The Moons and Esbats

The material below includes each particular month and its related moons and Esbats. Notice that the Esbats follow the Wheel of the Year and the associated season.

January Wolf Moon

After Yule, the first moon is known as The Wolf Moon. The Wolf, or hungry wolf, applies because this moon occurs in the middle of the cold season with death and desolation present. A hungry wolf takes the weak, and this time often focuses on endings, but also beginnings. This is a good time to do inner work to reflect on what you want to germinate for the upcoming spring.

What you will need:

- God box (box with a slit for receiving slips of paper)
- High quality ink in the primary colors of red, blue, green, and yellow . . . and black ink.
- Essential oil (I suggest Myrrh)
- Quill pen, or fountain pen (Something to use with the ink)
- Virgin paper (this is paper has *not* been used for any other purpose)

* * *

January Esbat

1) Cast the Circle (See Appendix)

2) *January Esbat Rite*

Take the essential oil, bottles of ink, and paper, and cleanse and consecrate them *(See Appendix)*.

Place three drops of the essential oil into each ink bottle and mix.

Set the bottles on the altar. Focus your energy into the bottles and say:

By my hand may these inks be blessed in the names of the God and Goddess to manifest my desires.

Set the bottles aside. Focus your energy into the virgin paper and say:

By my hand may this paper be blessed in the names of the God and Goddess to manifest my desires.

Sit and meditate on what you want to bring into your life in the coming year.

Once you have done this, take the quill (or fountain pen).

Choose the magickal ink you prefer and write a list of the things you desire to come to fruition.

Place the list into the God Box.

After the ritual, place the box in a safe place where it will not be disturbed.

3) Do the Cakes and Wine Ceremony (See Appendix)
4) Close the Circle (See Appendix)

* * * * * *

February Chaste Moon

February has the Chaste Moon, and this is the time the Goddess transitions back to the Maiden. At this time of the year, the Goddess readies Herself for the fertile role of Spring.

Also, at this time Wiccans focus on cleansing away unwanted energies; many clear away emotional and physical clutter.

* * *

February Esbat

What you will need:
- Paper in three small slips
- Pens (that you consecrated for the January Esbat; you have reserved these pens only for magickal purposes)
- Cauldron with a heat proof surface to place it on.

1) Cast the Circle (See Appendix)
2) *Clearing Clutter Meditation*

Relax. Take a deep breath. Breathe out; releasing the stresses of the day. Keep breathing deeply, in and out. With each exhale you're more and more relaxed. Feel each part of your body relax as deep comfort fills you. The light slowly dims. Feel comfortable and at peace as the light dims lower and lower. Now the light is gone and you are happy and secure in the darkness.

(Short pause)

The light returns, slowly at first. Then the full light reveals that you sit comfortably inside the Witch's Cottage. The air is fresh and clean.

Rise and walk toward the table. You see three old items resting on it. These items represent things you no longer need or desire to have in your life.

Look toward the left portion of the table. See one old item. What is it and what does it represent in your life that you no longer need?

(2 minute pause)

Look to the middle of the table and identify the second old item. What is it and what does this item represent in your life that you no longer need?

(2 minute pause)

Look to the right portion of the table and see the third old item. What is it and what does the item represent in your life that you no longer need?

(2 minute pause)

Step away from the table and choose a comfortable place to sit. The light slowly dims. You feel comfortable and at peace as the light dims lower and lower. Now the light is gone and you are happy and secure in the darkness.

(Short pause)

The light returns. Slowly at first. Then as your eyes adjust to the new light you now can see that you are back here safe and calm.

Cleanse and consecrate the three strips of paper. On the first strip of paper, write down the first item that you no longer need; also write down what this item represents for you. Focus your attention on this item and remind yourself that you no longer need it in your life. Using the working candle, set aflame this first strip of paper. Safely place the burning strip of paper into the cauldron. Watch it burn, knowing this item is leaving your life.

Write the second item down on the second strip of paper. Also write what this item represents for you. Focus your attention on this item and remind yourself that you no longer need it in your life. Using the working candle, set aflame this second strip of paper. Safely place the burning strip of paper into the cauldron. Watch it burn, knowing this item is leaving your life.

Write the third item down on the third strip of paper. Also write what this item represents for you. Focus your attention on this item and remind yourself that you no longer need it in your life. Using the working candle, set aflame this first strip of paper. Safely place the burning strip of paper into the cauldron. Watch it burn, knowing this item is leaving your life.

3) Do the Cakes and Wine Ceremony (See Appendix)
4) Close the Circle (See Appendix)

* * * * * *

March Seed Moon

As its name suggests, the Seed Moon is all about potential. Both physical and mental seeds can be readied for Spring. You can take physical seeds and start them indoors or you can take your mental seeds (desires) and plant them in your fertile mind. At this time, we focus on beginnings.

We will be making sigils as we do the March Esbat Ritual. Below is an example of a Success Sigil.

In order to conduct the March Esbat Ritual, here is what you will need:

- Magical inks
- Virgin paper (paper that hasn't been used for any other purpose)

- Quill or fountain pen
- Seeds for something you will plant (perhaps, corn, squash, peppers, or any other vegetable that you will eat later in the year)

* * *

March Esbat

1) Cast the Circle (See Appendix)

2) *March Esbat Rite*

Cleanse and consecrate the paper (See Appendix). Now pause and answer this question: What do you want to bring into your life this year? A new job or home?

Think about it, and once you have your desire picked out, write it down as a word or phrase.

Write your desire as a positive word or phrase such as "I attract X to me" or "X comes to me easily."

Cross out all the repeated letters until you have only one of each letter. Combine these few remaining letters into an image. (It's almost like drawing a picture.) Once your image is complete, set this image (your sigil) on your altar.

Concentrate on your new sigil and its meaning.

[For more about making a sigil, please refer to the section *How to Make Your Own Personal Sigils*—at the beginning of this book.]

Next, cleanse and consecrate the seeds.

3) Do the Cakes and Wine Ceremony (See Appendix)

4) Close the Circle (See Appendix)

After you complete the ritual, place your sigil and the

seeds in a safe location where they will not be disturbed. The idea is that the seeds absorb the energy from your sigil.

* * * * * *

April Hare Moon / Thunder Moon

At this time, Wiccans focus on fertility and new growth. During this ritual you will plant the seeds you used during the Seed Moon ritual.

The Hare Moon celebrates fertility. (Of course, hares are well-known for making many little hares.) It's about this time when things start to bud and grow.

What you will need:

- Seeds (from your Seed Moon ritual)
- Potting soil
- Pots or containers for planting your seeds

* * *

April Esbat

1) Cast the Sacred Circle (See Appendix)

2) *April Esbat Rite*

(Before the ritual, be sure to place the potting soil in the pots/containers in which you'll plant your seeds.)

Think about what you want to manifest in your life in the coming year. Hold up one seed and concentrate on your desire. Say:

Little seed as you grow so my desire "Name of Desire" grows.

Plant the seed in a container.

This can be repeated as many times you want. Go around until everyone has completed the process of planting and expressing their own affirmation.

Place the planted seeds in their containers in the middle of the circle and dance around them, concentrating on your desires.

3) Do the Cakes and Wine Ceremony (See Appendix)
4) Close the Circle (See Appendix)

* * * * * *

May Dryad Moon

During the time of The Dryad Moon, you can see some growth in the seeds you have planted. You can also plant seedlings of your desires in your heart and mind.

What you will need:
- Spade to dig holes for the seedlings.
- Plant food.
- Bucket of water

* * *

May Esbat

1) Cast the Circle (See Appendix)
2) *May Esbat Rite*

Place your athame into the water and envision a white light that blesses the water. [Be sure to *not* place salt into the water because such salt will harm your plants.]

Last month, you placed seedlings in little containers. During this ritual you will gently remove the plants from the containers and place them into holes you prepare in the ground.

Gently take each seedling out and plant it in the ground,

giving it a small offering of plant food. Then water the seedling saying:

As you grow so does "Name of desire" grow and becomes manifest.

3) Do the Cakes and Wine Ceremony (See Appendix).
4) Close the Circle (See Appendix).

* * *

June Mead Moon / Honey Moon

Wonder why this moon is sometimes called the Honey Moon? The flowers have bloomed, and the bees have made honey. This is a time of love, marriage and success.

At this time you tend your garden whose seeds have now become happy plants. Further, by this time, a number of your desires have probably grown into opportunities.

For decades, Pagans have chosen this time to brew mead. What you will need:

- Plant food (if you need to re-fertilize your plants)
- Bottle of water
- Wand
- Music for dancing

* * *

June Esbat

1) Cast the Circle (See the Appendix)
2) *June Esbat Ritual*

Place the bottle of water and plant food on the altar. Bless the water in the bottle. (Later you can add the blessed water to a bucket of water The idea is that a small amount of the blessed water will thus bless the bucket of water.)

Asperge and cense the plant food and bottle of water.

(Note: When you bless the water do **not** use the method of adding salt; salt will harm your plants.)

Hold your wand over the bottle of water and plant food and say:

Water of life, bless and nurture the growth of what I desire. Food of life, nurture and nourish the growth of my desire "Name of desire."

Turn on your music player and dance to the music while focusing on the above words. And focus your energy on the water and plant food. At the end of the musical piece, complete your dance.

Go to your garden or other location where you planted your seedlings the previous month.

Water each seedling using the bottled water.

If you have a lot of seedlings to water, you can use a small portion of blessed water and add it to a bucket of water for continued watering of your garden.

Remember the plants are helping your desires blossom and grow. So make sure the plants are healthy.

Each healthy plant makes your desire more likely to manifest. Give your plants plant food and water. Tie them to trellises if they need support.

3) Do the Cakes and Wine Ceremony (See Appendix).
4) Close the Circle (See Appendix).

* * *

July Wort Moon

Wiccans celebrate the Wort Moon as the time for agriculture and abundance. We enjoy the beginning fruits of our labors. Our intentions that we set during the Seed Moon are now in full swing.

What you will need:

- The first fruits of your garden or the first seasonal produce from your local farmers market
- Barbeque grill or pit fire
- Meat of choice (optional)
- Music appropriate for summer

Note: This ritual should be done outside (for barbequing)

Preparation: Prepare vegetables and meat for barbequing. You can make kebabs or cut the veggies into large slices (so that the slices do not fall through the grill).

You can marinate the meat in the fresh herbs of the season that you may have collected from your garden. Place the food to be barbequed on the altar.

The July Esbat is a good ritual for one's family or coven on a nice Saturday afternoon.

* * * * * *

July Esbat

1) Cast the Circle (See Appendix)

2) *July Esbat Rite*

Bless and consecrate the food (See Appendix).

Play your music selection on your music player. Have all conveners form a conga line with the High Priest and High Priestess holding the food in the lead. Conga around the altar and then to the barbeque grill.

High Priest and High Priestess hold up food to be cooked and say:

Behold the bounty of the first harvest of summer. The

God and Goddess lovingly provide for their children once again.

Cook the food on the grill and then give some food to each person as you say:
You are blessed by the God and Goddess. Partake of their bounty. Blessed be.

3) Do the Cakes and Wine Ceremony (See Appendix)
4) Close the Circle (See Appendix)

* * * * * *

August Barley Moon

August includes the time of the Barley Moon when the first harvests take place. The grains have ripened, and farmers begin reaping what they have sown.

What you will need:
- The physical harvest from your garden (perhaps, vegetables, herbs or something else)
- The metaphorical harvest of what you desire (perhaps, in the Spring you "planted the seeds" for better relationships or a new, better job).
- Loaf of sourdough bread
- Olive oil (Take herbs like parsley and rosemary, and use a mortar and pestle to grind them up and set them in the oil). It's best to do this in advance so that the flavors mingle.
- Grill or cook your harvest vegetables.
- A mortar and pestle

* * *

August Esbat

1) Cast the Circle (See Appendix)

2) *August Esbat Rite*

Bless and consecrate the herb oil (see Appendix). Place the herb oil in a pan and cook the vegetables harvested from your garden. Place the cooked vegetables in a bowl upon your altar along with the loaf of bread and extra herb oil (in a small bottle).

One at a time each person holds up his or her cooked harvested vegetables and says:

As I eat this [name of plant to be consumed], so my desires for [specific desire] become manifest in my life.

Each person then consumes part or all of their cooked harvested vegetables.

High Priest: holds up the bread and says:

As this bread represents me, I sacrifice myself so that my children may live.

High Priest then slices the bread and gives each covener a piece of the bread.

High Priest holds up the bottle of herb oil and says:

I give the fruits of my life to my children.

High Priest pours herb oil into a bowl.

Each covener then dips the bread into the herb oil and eats it saying:

Hail the God of the harvest.

3) Do the Cakes and Wine Ceremony (See Appendix)

4) Close the Circle (See Appendix)

* * * * * *

September Wine Moon

Wiccans celebrate the second harvest during The Wine Moon. You celebrate the bounty in your life. The seeds and intentions you set in the Spring will be coming into maturity.

What you will need:

- Sigils you made in March
- Caldron and a heatproof surface

Note: We will be burning our sigils as an offering of thanks to the Gods for their help in manifesting our desires.

(For more about sigils, see the section *How to Make Your Own Personal Sigils* at the beginning of this book).

What if our desires have not been met? Then keep your sigils for the final and last harvest at Samhain (in October). In the meantime, wait to see if they fulfill themselves at Samhain.

* * *

September Esbat

1) Cast the Circle (See Appendix)

2) *September Esbat Rite*

As you take a sigil in your hand, say:

I thank the Gods for helping me grant my [name of your desire].

Gaze at the sigil and envision the accomplished desire with thanks in your heart.

Light the sigil with the flame of the working candle. Place the burning sigil carefully into the cauldron for safe burning.

Make sure the sigil burns completely.

If you have multiple sigils repeat the process until all have been burned in the cauldron.

3) Do the Cakes and Wine Ceremony (See Appendix)
4) Close the Circle (See Appendix)

* * * * * *

October Blood Moon / Harvest Moon

Wiccans celebrate the time of the last harvest as The Blood Moon or Harvest Moon. As the final harvests come in from the fields, Wiccans cull any unwanted attributes in their life. This is the best time for divination and talking to the other side.

What you will need:

- Next year's calendar. (You will be looking for the full moons and the Sabbats.)
- Pencil or pen.
- Pad of paper.
- Tarot deck of your choice.

Note: If you didn't receive your desire by now, the Gods may have something else in store for you. If you have received your desire by now repeat the September Esbat.

* * *

October Esbat

1) Cast the Circle (See Appendix)
2) *October Esbat Rite*
Take only the Major Arcana* cards and mix those cards separately from the rest of the deck. This deck will now be called "The Major Arcana Deck."
[*Major Arcana cards are defined as 0-21 a total of 22. These

cards are not part of the four suits (Pentacles/Coins, Cups, Wands/Staves, and Swords). The four suits make up the minor arcana.]

Next, gather the calendar, pad of paper and your pen/pencil. Go through the calendar and note the date of each event (Sabbat, Esbat). Write these down in order on your pad of paper.

Be sure to leave space below each event so that you can write notes about what you discover in your reading of the Tarot cards. [You will do an actual Tarot reading for the whole year.]

Shuffle the cards of the Major Arcana Deck. Spread the cards across the table facedown. Now pull a random card out of the middle of the spread.

Place this card to your far left on the table. Take a second random card and place it to the right side of the first card. Keep up this process until you have all 22 cards in a row — all face up.

Start with the far left card. You will next write down your impressions on your pad. As you look at this first card, allow your intuition to serve up some first impressions. Write these impressions down in the first slot of the first Esbat of the year.

Take the next card. Note your intuitive impressions and write them down in the slot (of the pad) for the next calendar event.

Continue this process until you have moved through the whole calendar and through the cards in succession. You notice that you have one card left. This card represents the theme of the year.

Through the above process, you will be able to divine the details of the events to come throughout the new year.

3) Do the Cakes and Wine Ceremony (See Appendix)
4) Close the Circle (See Appendix)

* * * * * *

November Oak Moon / Hunter Moon

Wiccans appreciate November as the time of the Oak Moon or Hunter Moon. At this time of year, our ancestors focused on hunting as their main means of survival. This is a time of introspection, attention to our blessings and gathering with our family and friends.

What you will need:
- Slips of paper
- Pen
- Magickal Ink
- Cauldron

* * *

November Esbat

1) Cast the Circle (See Appendix)

2) *November Esbat Rite*

High Priest and High Priestess ask all: **"What have you been thankful for this year?"**

The High Priest and High Priestess guide a group discussion on the above topic.

Next, each covener blesses and consecrates his or her personal slips of paper (See Appendix).

Now recalling what they spoke of during the group discussion, each covener writes down (using magickal ink) something she or he feels thankful for. Concentrate on being thankful as you write down the item.

After filling out their slips of paper, each covener takes one slip of paper says:

I am thankful to the God and Goddess for my blessing.

The Coven Member ignites the slip of paper on the flame of the working candle and carefully places the burning item into the caldron.

The Coven Member envisions his or her gratitude rising as the smoke floats up toward the Gods.

The Coven Members each take one turn with one slip of paper. This process continues until all have ignited all of their slips of paper.

3) Do the Cakes and Wine Ceremony (See Appendix)
4) Close the Circle (See Appendix)

* * * * * *

December Snow Moon

Wiccans traditionally look upon this time as when the world is covered in a deep blanket of snow. Wiccans celebrate this time of birth and rebirth. This is when we see the "light side" of the year return. We envision new seeds for the Spring.

What you will need:
- Cauldron
- Heat-proof surface for the cauldron
- Sea Salt or Kosher salt
- Rubbing alcohol

Preparation: Take the cauldron and place salt inside, then add a bit of the alcohol (Be careful to avoid spilling the alcohol.) Place the cauldron on the heat-proof surface.

* * *

December Esbat

1) Cast the Circle (See Appendix)

Everyone now sits around the cauldron facing it. High Priestess then lights the taper and then uses it to light the cauldron's mixture and say:

As the Goddess's womb renews and offers re-birth, so this flame offers new insights to us for the New Year.

2) *December Esbat Meditation*

Relax. Take a deep breath in. Breathe out, releasing the stresses of the day. Keep taking deep breaths, in and out. With each exhale you get more and more relaxed. Feel your body as it sits comfortably Notice now that the light slowly begins to dim. You feel comfortable and at peace as the light continues to fade. Now the light is gone and you are happy and secure in the darkness.

(Short pause)

Soon you notice the light starts to return. Slowly at first, it blooms around you. As your eyes adjust to the new light, you see that you are in the Witch's Cottage. The air is fresh and clean. Go to the door leading to the outside and greet the Guardian. The Guardian acknowledges you with a nod, and lets you pass as you step onto the porch. It is a nice clear day, and you smell the plants that grow around the Cottage. You see a path in front of you; it stretches away from the cottage. Walk down the path. Soon you come to a gate at the border of your piece of land that surrounds the Cottage. Go through the gate, and enter a pasture. The path continues for several yards, and you walk it easily.

(Short pause)

You arrive at a fork in the path, graced by a large Oak tree, a lone sentinel on the path before you. At the fork, you see one path to the left and the other to the right. Take the left path and go towards a hill you see in the distance. You find the walk to the hill easy and enjoyable.

(1 minute pause)

Stand at the base of the hill. You see a shape at the top. It is not distinct, but it invites you to come closer. Climb upwards to see what it is.

(Short pause)

You finally reach the top and see a Stone Circle. Now step through the gateway of the Stone Circle.

(Short pause)

Stand in the middle of the Stone Circle where it is peaceful and quiet. You see a stone altar which has a cauldron with a blue flame in it.

The blue flame casts a gentle light on the stones around you. The blue flame represents the potential you have for the future. Kneeling before the altar, you now close your eyes and meditate on where you want to go in the coming year.

(3 minute pause)

Having received your answers, you open your eyes. Rise to your feet and turn toward the gateway. Pass through the gateway and back onto the path. Walk down the hill and continue on the path to the Cottage.

(Short pause)

The walk is easy and soon you come back to the old Oak Tree.

(Short pause)

Keep walking and arrive at the gate of your piece of land that surrounds the Cottage. Pass through the gate and continue on to the Cottage Door where the Guardian stands, waiting. Greet the Guardian. The Guardian nods in acknowledgment and lets you enter. Now inside the Witch's Cottage, find a nice place and sit. Rest a while. Then notice how the light starts dimming. Feel comfortable and at peace as the light continues to fade. Now the light is gone and you are happy and secure in the darkness.

(Short pause)

Soon you notice that the light starts to return. Slowly at first. Your eyes adjust to the new light and you feel safe, calm and refreshed. Now open your eyes to your present-day world.

3) Do the Cakes and Wine Ceremony (See Appendix).
4) Close the Circle (See Appendix).

* * *

Now that you've experienced this chapter, you can see how Wiccans celebrate their connection with the God and Goddess throughout the year.

Moonwater SilverClaw

CHAPTER 7:
MONEY, SECURITY AND WISDOM

Is Money Spiritual?

Have you heard in some form that "money is not spiritual"?

Some of us have heard a misquote that goes "Money is the root of all evil."

(Actually, the correct quote is: "The *love* of money is the root of all evil.")

There's a real problem: ignoring money or actually looking down on having money causes unhappiness. Some say that having denial about money issues causes many people to end up poor and unable to take care of their own basic needs.

In Wicca we know our Gods want us to be happy. With this as true, does it make sense that our lacking money is what they want? No. Now I'm not saying that you need to be making buckets of money or that it's necessary to have a whole lot more than you need.

But for many in our community money is elusive. Why?

For a number of individuals, Wicca was not their first taste of spirituality. They may come from different faiths that look down upon having money. The horrible part is that debilitating beliefs about money often stick in a person's subconscious mind. And these sick beliefs push them to be unhappy.

Let's go back to the misquote that goes "Money is the root of all evil."

Is it money? No, *fear* is the root of all evil.

Think of it. Fear pushes us toward greed. Fear of never having enough. I remember the famous line from *Gone with the Wind:* "I will never be hungry again!" In that film, Scarlett O'Hara does extreme things because of her huge fear of being hungry or losing her property.

Is it possible that having money can frighten us? Yes, that can be a problem. Some of us have been conditioned to think that rich people are money-obsessed and that they do bad things. So on a subconscious level, some people are afraid of losing themselves and actually avoid opportunities to become rich and successful. Again, I call these sick beliefs.

Some of us are really afraid of having money. It continues to come from subconscious beliefs drilled into our heads that having and/or obtaining money is not spiritual.

In contrast to this above limiting belief, I suggest that having and/or obtaining money *is* spiritual. Money creates opportunities for us to be happy. It creates safety for us and our families. The Gods want us to feel this way. Though this is not quite a Wiccan belief I feel it would actually help us live better.

If we're doing well with our personal money situation, we walk around with an air of positive energy. We can be compassionate to others. Expressing compassion is an important part of our spiritual path.

We have many ways of creating prosperity. Just doing money spells is not the full answer.

Ideally, we would use magick to get to an inner state where we can work out problems that prevent us from enjoying financial abundance. We can do meditations and inner work to change the limiting thought patterns and beliefs we have about money. (For more about this, see a free chapter on Amazon.com from my book, *The Hidden Children of the Goddess*.)

Some Wiccans may default to doing prosperity spells to gain money. However, it may help *more* for you to do a *healing spell* to dissolve any blocks to learning how to earn more money, save money and *improve spending habits*.

Let's start with new and empowering thoughts about money. For example, author Jason Miller talks about the difference between *rich* and *wealth*. I think he says it well:

"A rich person has a high income, which is a stream that can feed being wealthy or being in debt, depending on how that money is used. There is no shortage of people with high incomes but no real wealth. . . . Wealth is not a flow of income; it is a state of positive finances."

What is a state of positive finances? Such a state includes enough money for bills, some money for entertainment, savings for tough situations in life, some money to be kind to others, and savings towards one's retirement. The state of positive finances is not about having just enough to barely get by. It is really about having some amount of financial abundance (more than enough).

To live in lack (including difficulties about money) really isn't the Gods' and Goddesses' plan for us. They invite us to grow, learn and adapt. They invite us to learn something about creating financial abundance.

Let's begin today.

With that being said, is money security? Yes, it can pave the way by giving you a roof over your head and food on the table, but what about true security?

How You Can Feel True Security

Security—what is it? Is it a home, a job, or family? If that's security, then what if these things are taken away? What then?

My friend Bob lives with his parents. He is disabled and can't manage to live on his own. He also needs the support of his family to help him with day-to-day activities such as cooking and cleaning. To him, his living situation with his family is a place of security. However, last week he was told by his father that he had to move out. This pulled the rug of security right out from under him.

Bob was terrified.

Here's another example: Janet has to keep her Wiccan faith a secret from her family who subscribe to another religion. One day, at a family gathering her pentacle pendent fell out of her blouse. Aghast, her mother called her father and together they yelled and drove her from the gathering. Her parents and other relatives disowned her. That was their word, *disowned*.

Now, Janet cries at different times during the day. Sometimes she flees to the restroom when she's at work. She used to believe that her family was her bedrock. No more.

What happens when our sense of security is taken? Where do we go? Did we really lose security?

I say security isn't a place. It's not a thing, and it's not a family tie. The truth is: Things change. We can't rely on these things for our security.

So where is security found?

True security is found in our hearts and minds. It is found in our faith, and it resides with the Gods who walk beside us everyday.

The Gods do not waver. They are constant, eternal, all encompassing.

So let's face it. Security is not in the material. True security is in the spirit.

You can call on your true security anytime and anyplace. The great thing about being Wiccan is that you can create your temple anywhere by casting your circle.

More than that, you can recite a blessing in your own thoughts.

Here is a blessing that you can recite to yourself:

Gods to enfold me, Gods that surround me.
Be that peace and serenity for me.
Lead me on my path, far and wide,
Traveling with me, by my side.
Never will I be alone,
Evermore you'll be my home.
Ever safe and secure I will always be,
Never bowing defeat upon one knee.
Lord and Gracious Lady be,
mine for all eternity.

So mote it be.

Remember your true security with the Gods.

* * *

Finding Your Way on the Sacred Path

Starting upon the Wiccan path for the first time is a big step. Finding *your way* is the next step.

So how did you find the Wiccan faith? Was it through a personal connection or was it through a book or website?

Wiccans until recently were hard to find. Many followers of the path work in secret, in the shadows. Why all the secrecy?

This secrecy was vital because throughout history, and even to this present day, Wiccans (and other pagans) have been and continue to be discriminated against.

Face it, we are still a minority faith in this world. Most practitioners prefer to stay in the shadows because of the possibility of retaliation and prejudice found in family, school, work, and the general public. We know too well that there are general misconceptions and fear about the Craft. So many Wiccans practice in the shadow. (After all, I call my blog and my first book *The Hidden Children of the Goddess*.)

So how can you find a reliable teacher when so many teachers practice in the shadows?

You need some initial education. Books like this one can be a great way to start. Read a bunch of books and you will start to see a pattern. Your intuition will alert you to who really knows valuable material and who may be offering faulty information. It's important to have a good foundation in the Craft before moving on to the more advanced practices.

Once you have read a number of books, you will have a basic familiarity with the Craft. Next, find a mentor in the particular Tradition (type) of Wicca you want to study.

The Witches' Voice (witchvox.com) is a great place to read more articles and to network for new connections. You can find people who have taken the giant step (and risks) to be known in the community.

Observe carefully. Use your basic familiarity with the Craft and your intuition to find someone who you feel is a good match for your next steps in learning.

Each Tradition does the Craft a little differently. It's not that one particular Tradition's ritual is "wrong" compared to another Tradition. There are many ways of doing the same thing correctly.

The Wiccan Path can be hard to traverse. Life comes at you with many problems. Sometimes these problems can seem almost impossible to solve. But we as Wiccans can deal with these problems in many ways.

How Do You Heal When Life Slams You With Too Much

My close friend was shot dead at his workplace a few days before I wrote this section of this book (Yule Time in 2013). I had just endured foot surgery, and I had family members upset in a current whirlwind of activities.

I just kept thinking, "What's next? All of this happening around the sacred Yule time. I'm squeezed by both emotional and physical pain, feeling overwhelmed."

Needing support at this time, I wrote this blessing to connect with the God and the Goddess. I knew my real feelings of being supported would arise from connecting with Them.

A Blessing for Comfort and Healing:
As the moon is high above me,
The Goddess is deep within me.
As the sun shines long and bright,
The God's compassion fills me right.

With broken heart and shattered dreams,
Black as night with all scary fiends.
Lord and Lady lift me up,
Let me drink from your healing cup.
Mending all my broken pieces,
Ironing out all my creases.
Mending all that was strewn about,
Healing all with no stone left out.

So mote it be.

Above, I shared a blessing for comfort and healing. We'll now continue with a blessing for success and strength.

A Blessing for Success and Strength

Are you walking the path you want to be traversing? Would you choose a different path? We're all walking a path at the moment. But the question is: Is this the path you prefer?

Years ago, I felt I had no control over the path of life I was walking on. I felt like I was just dragged along, whether I enjoyed it or not.

Many of us feel like that, at least some of the time. How do we take control of our path? One thing that helps is meditation. This clears the mind of the distractions and helps us focus on the important elements of life.

For a little extra help you can say this blessing upon yourself.

A Blessing for Success and Strength

I call upon the power of the Gods and the mighty ones that I may be blessed.

*Blessed be my **mind**, that it be clear of all distractions, focused on its sacred purpose.*

*Blessed be my **eyes**, that they see without hate and that they see my correct path.*

*Blessed be my **lips** that they speak with strength, beauty, kindness and truth.*

*Blessed be my **voice**, that it be clear and strong and that it not shake in fear from adversity or from facing closed minds.*

*Blessed be my **heart**, that I always have love and compassion for myself and others.*

*Blessed be my **arms**, that they carry my burdens with strength and ease.*

*Blessed be my **hands**, that they work and create with purpose, steadily and honorably.*

*Blessed be my **knees** that they not tremble with fear when hardships come my way.*

*Blessed be my **feet** that they do not waver, but walk on the sacred path of light with surefootedness and purpose.*

I have found that using empowering words in meditation is helpful to turn the direction of one's thoughts.

What words do you use to empower yourself?

Another way to empowerment is listening to our elders in our community. We can learn how our elders traveled their own path. We can gain insight and avoid some pitfalls on our personal path.

How Wicca Values Wisdom

Have you ever felt bothered by how media pushes that people need to be "young and beautiful"?

You may have noticed that Wicca pushes back against media in that Wicca honors and respects our elders.

Have you also noticed how the Western World seems to overlook the merits of tempered wisdom and instead favors youth?

Wicca acknowledges that for our species, youth is life. Youth is fertility and health. Wicca also acknowledges that, as one lives, wisdom can blossom. Wisdom arose as early people learned which berries were safe to eat and which plants could heal. With wisdom we not only survived, we thrived. Wicca acknowledges the value of both youth and elders' wisdom. Elders have traveled the path of life ahead of us. They can help us do better on our personal path if we care to listen.

Just like youthful strong bodies can get hard work done, elders have the wisdom of knowing how to work smart.

This is important for survival.

In past eras, without the wisdom of the elders, people couldn't survive. Because of this, we valued our elders.

However, as time has passed, technology has seemed to make elders' advice and experience less relevant. With life moving as fast as it does, many of us would rather read something on the Internet than talk to an elder. I get that. I love tech; I'm a blogger after all. But with all the bells and whistles technology has, we still need our humanity for us to really learn.

It's like reading about the Titanic disaster in a book as opposed to actually talking with a survivor who lived through the experience. The survivor will be able to tell you the visceral experience they had along with other crucial information that a book just can't convey.

We pick up so much in nonverbal cues: the look on a person's face, the tonality of their voice, and the pace in which they speak.

Think of it: Storytelling has been such a valuable part of humanity's life. We learn so much because we actually *experience the truth of a situation* while we experience a *person telling a story.*

In the Western World we have forgotten the important distinction of experience versus merely reading some facts conveyed in a barren form on the Internet.

The good news is: Wiccans—like a number of Eastern cultures—have retained wisdom. As Wiccans, we understand that we need both the vitality and virility of youth, but it must be tempered with the wisdom and knowledge of age in order for us to survive and enhance our path in life.

Wiccans know that to travel a spiritual path you need wisdom to know where to tread and where not to tread. Elders can talk with you about life, if not current technology. They can talk with you about the people who make technology. They can provide the patience and understanding about tough issues like loss and grief. They can even help you appreciate the joys of life.

I invite you to consider elders as another resource. They can guide you in ways that something you read just can't.

Wiccans know that there is more to life than tech. Some wisdom and learning comes only from having lived through tough experiences.

See how you might connect with appropriate elders.

You'll find new facets of life opening to you.

Elders sometimes remind us of ways to bring more joy and peace to our lives.

And sometimes, we have a new experience that sheds new light on our path.

Helping the Goddess

My friend, John, drives the lead car and I follow in mine. We're going on a camping trip. This one will be different: we're going "disperse camping," that is, we're not using a public campground. I'm tired, but there's hope! John flicks his blinker on and we turn off the road. *Finally*, no more driving. We step out of our cars and look around. The site turns my stomach.

There is trash *everywhere*, whole bags of it strewn across the forest, even a latrine. Yuck! Some campers just left all their trash; it had to have been quite a large group by how much trash was still there.

What would you do in this situation?

We had the option to find another spot. But as a Wiccan, I have a duty to Mother Earth.

Clearing some of the garbage we managed to set up camp. Then we drove to the ranger station down the road and told the rangers of the deplorable conditions of the site.

Then we did something they weren't expecting. We asked for garbage bags so that we could clean up the site. Their shocked but pleased faces told the story. They were quite happy to give us as many bags as we wanted.

Back at the camp site, we picked up the garbage along the river and then moved on to the camp area.

Six large and very full trash bags later, the site looked much better. I could feel the Goddess smiling.

On the other hand, it truly saddens me that some people could do this to their Mother.

As witches, Wiccans and pagans, we care for our mother. With this attitude much of our community cherishes an opportunity to clean Mother Earth.

You don't have to look far and wide for such an opportunity. Just walk your own neighborhood. Or go to a local park. You'll find plenty to clean and improve.

I personally feel a duty to keep my Mother clean and healthy.

How about you?

This is another way to show the Gods respect and love.

You'll feel better, too.

Speaking of feeling better, sometimes we feel that we're too tired to cast circle and do a ritual. Sometimes, that's true. And other times, we'll find more energy when we *do a ritual.*

Discover The Deep Truth Beneath Casting Circle and Ritual

I just couldn't get my mind to settle down. My friend's suicide happened, and it really tore at my heart. I knew that I had to make sure that he transitioned safely to the Summerlands. The transition just wasn't going to happen on its own. That's what the Tarot told me.

So I pushed myself and took action. I did a ritual to help him find the Summerlands. Once I knew he had crossed safely, I felt peace in my heart.

For Wiccans, we do have a source of relief and even deep peace: Ritual.

In my studies, I've learned that Ritual is designed to get us free of the conscious mind and its petty obsessions.

The more often that you Cast a Circle, Conduct Ritual, Do the Cakes and Wine Ceremony and Close the Circle, you become *stronger*.

You become conditioned to go to a Higher Level where you can open the unconscious mind and open the doors to successful magick.

Successful magick happens when you open those doors wide and do it reliably. Repetition of rituals is the best way to change your consciousness so that you can do magick reliably.

The more often you do ritual, the more you train your mind to make a transition to a Higher Level.

Each ritual begins with Casting a Circle. When you cast a circle you not only set up your sacred space with related protection, but your casting also opens those doors to your subconscious mind, which is called the Younger Self. We Wiccans use the Younger Self for communication as we do magick. By the way, the Younger Self is also known as the Sticky Self in the faerie tradition.

You might think of your Younger Self as a five-year-old. How do you keep a five-year-old engaged? Not with long-winded talking. Instead, you use things like props and other items. Think shiny, sparkly with loud noises.

Using drums, other musical instruments and other props that are fun and novel will help you easily communicate with the Younger Self.

Wiccans realize the Younger Self is the source of energy for effectively doing magick.

Remember that regularly doing ritual helps you condition

yourself to readily rise to a Higher Level and engage your Younger Self. In this way, your magick-work will get better.

CHAPTER 8:
MAGICK AND MORE TO HELP YOU COPE
AND GROW

Imagine feeling stronger as you continue on the Wiccan path. Personal growth is a vital part of the Wiccan path. This is why I love it so. Much of what you will find in this chapter helped me stay on track or helped me have the tools to change my life for the better. One of the major things I need to keep in mind, as I am sure many others do, is to keep the connection. The following expresses that.

Keep the Connection

My muscles ache and I'm wobbly on my feet. My Dad and I walk on a wooded trail in Pinecrest, California. My only thought is: Can I make it to the car?

On the drive back to our campsite, I think, *I really need to go hiking more often. My muscles are just not in the condition I'd like them to be in.*

Without enough hiking I lose valuable muscle mass and tone. And, without enough vigorous exercise, I'll lose bone mass or even get a "flabby" heart, a cause of other health problems.

How does this connect with Wicca? We see something similar: without enough practice, you can lose your competency in the Wiccan path. Just as muscles become weaker due to lack of use, so does your proficiency in Wicca.

Out of practice in Wicca, your spells will not be as effective. They can even go bad because you're failing to channel your energy to your desired goal. Such errors can cause undesired effects.

Fail to practice your faith and you may separate from nature which Wiccans hold so sacred. If you don't pay attention to the cycles of nature (the cycles of life and the seasons), you may lose compassion for others who are going through personal cycles of growth and sometimes personal pain. Human beings live in a cycle of puberty, aging and other personal challenges.

Separating from nature, you may even lose compassion for yourself.

On the other hand, you can be diligent in your practice. You can exercise your Wiccan muscle just as you would support your body through physical exercise.

When your "Wiccan muscles" are in tune, you'll take good care of yourself and stay aware of the *Three Times Law* (you get back three times what you put out in the world).

Be good to your spirit like you're good to your body through exercise.

Keep a diligent practice, and you become stronger and calmer. You have more patience.

So let's flex all of our muscles to be both spiritually and physically healthy.

Keeping up your diligent practice can really help when you're confronted with the tough parts of life.

Looking Within and Finding Control in Your Life

I'm gasping for breath in the ER, yet again, hit by my asthma. I'm hearing a man on meth scream at the top of his lungs in Spanish. I wonder when the doctor will come and help me. I'm thinking, "Please don't put me on prednisone again."

I have been on prednisone three times in the past month and a half. Each time I've gained significant weight because of the medication.

I seem to be losing my battle of the bulge. *I just want to be healthy.*

Losing weight would help me in so many ways. Not only would my body be happy but my mind would also be free from the burden of worrying about diabetes. I'd just be happy to move easily.

So why is it not in my cards?

The meth-man behind the curtain wrenches at his restraints and screams profanities in Spanish. That's when it hits me . . .

I'm the screaming man. I'm in a situation I cannot control, tethered to my asthma, angry as hell.

The doctor comes in and orders two nebulizer treatments and puts me back on prednisone. Again!

I can't stop my asthma; it is something I don't control.

So what can I control?

1. What goes in my body.

Yes, I need strong medications. But I can control my intake of food and drink. I'll eat what the God and Goddess provide such as natural vegetables and fruits instead of artificial foods. (Donuts are my bane.)

2. Moving my body.

Yes, it is more difficult to exercise; it's hard to breathe. But I can move some each day. It doesn't have to be overtaxing so that I have an asthma attack. Any movement is good. Walking in the beauty of the world that the Gods have created is good for us, and the Gods especially like it when we appreciate their handiwork.

3. Getting rest.

Getting rest to heal is just as important as movement. Getting adequate rest lessens my asthma problems. I am going to increase time for meditation, which will soothe my brain, body and soul.

Feeling some comfort.

Understanding I have power in these three areas is comforting. I can't control the side effects of the drugs I take. *But there are things I can do.*

Concentrating on what I can do in these three areas raises my morale. I can practice letting go of worries about what I cannot control.

This brings moments of happiness to my daily life.

I invite you to look at the two areas: What can you control? And what is completely out of your control?

When you get clear about these distinctions and you bring your efforts to the Gods, you'll find some comfort.

You deserve it.

When you're looking for comfort, sometimes it's really tough, especially if something brings up the fear of death.

How You Can Let Go of Fearing Death

Do you fear death? Do you wonder what awaits you on

the other side?

Several years ago, in the hospital, I was at death's door. I had Idiopathic Thrombocytopenic Purpura (ITP). ITP is a bleeding disorder which can cause a person to bleed out simply by bumping into furniture. I could hemorrhage in my brain at any time and die instantly. When my dentist saw bruising inside my mouth, he told me to *immediately go to the Emergency Room.* (I'm returning to this topic because it made such an impact on me.)

With ITP, the immune system destroys platelets, which are necessary for normal blood clotting.

Without normal blood clotting, I was at death's door. After the first night I stayed at the hospital, the next morning I had bruises all down my body from lying on the bed. I had to remain sitting even while I slept. Because my brain could have hemorrhaged and killed me, I got to know death's call intimately. Death was there everyday, sitting by my side waiting with me.

I had to accept that death could take me at anytime.

At first I was afraid. But then I realized that death is just a transition, not an ending.

Death is a transition to the Summerlands, a wonderful place of comfort and peace. Your family and friends who went before are there. Who could fear that?

When I first heard of the Summerlands, a complete knowing came to me. I also realized that that this place of comfort and peace is where we came from. So you don't need to fear returning to where you came from. When we die, we go home.

Once you return home, you can choose to be born again. Wiccans know this as reincarnation.

So as you connect with the idea and reality of the Summerlands, you can let go of fears about dying. Death is simply a transition to a place of rest, loved ones and renewal to prepare you for the next life, if you so choose.

Understanding that now, I do not fear death.

* * *

Finding peace is one of the things I love most about the craft. Magick is another. We can help ourselves and guide our life's outcomes with it. Here is a tool that has worked for me. It has literally placed thousands of dollars in my pockets.

Magickal Alphabets – The Theban Alphabet

Imagine writing down your spells so that a casual observer would *not* be able to decipher your notes. Nowadays, someone could look up the characters, but they'd have to put some effort into it. The unusual writing form I'm talking about is the Theban Alphabet. Several years ago, when I was in college, I found the Theban Alphabet referenced in a book.

I loved the beauty of script lines. To learn this beautiful alphabet, I started writing my college lecture notes in Theban.

Where did the magickal Theban Alphabet come from? In the medieval period, magick workers wanted to disguise their notes. A number of forms of magickal writings were developed, including Theban. Then and now, alchemical and other occult traditions use Theban.

Today, the Theban Alphabet is still used in paganism and especially in witchcraft. The letters in English and their equivalent Theban representatives are in the below image:

Symbol	Letter	Symbol	Letter
ʎ = A		ʰₘ = N	
ꟼ = B		ꟽ = O	
ᵚ = C		ᵚ = P	
ᵚ = D		ꟼ = Q	
ꟲ = E		ᵚ = P	
ᵚ = F		ꟼ = Q	
ᵚ = G		ᵚ = R	
ꟼ = H		ᵚ = S	
ᵁ = I		ᵚ = T	
ᵁ = J		ꟼ = U	
ᵚ = K		ꟼ = V	
ᵚ = L		ꟼꟼ = W	
ᵚ = M		ᵁᵐ = X	
The End of		ꟽₘ = Y	
a Sentence		ꟽₕ = Z	

Several magick workers use Theban to keep their secrets. Only those who were initiated or taught this script could pry the magickal secrets from the pages of the writer.

So how might you use the Theban Alphabet? Consider using the script for writing in your Book of Shadows (BOS). Gerald B. Gardner wrote much of his magickal texts in Theban.

You can use Theban for talismans, carving on candles and much of the magickal work that you do.

Got a Magickal name? Use Theban to write it out. Make a personal sigil by using the Theban letters. Check out my Sigils post to know more about making Sigils.

I must say, writing in Theban can be fun.

In any case, you may want to write in some special script to elevate how you write as part of your magickal workings.

CONCLUSION

We have discovered many ways of caring for ourselves and walking the sacred path. I have shown you some of my own processes and what I have learned during my own journey.

Now, I invite your to continue on your path. What have you learned? Where will your path lead you?

We never stop learning as we walk the path. We walk it all our life and into the next. The path can be challenging at times, making us work for our knowledge.

I find that the harder I work walking on my own path, the more I learn.

May you learn much and enjoy your path.

Blessings,
Moonwater SilverClaw

P.S. If you have questions or comments I would love to hear from you. Askawitchnow@gmail.com

ABOUT THE AUTHOR

Moonwater SilverClaw is a Wiccan High Priestess and member of the Covenant of the Goddess and the New Wiccan Church. She has trained people new to Wicca. Her personal story reveals how Wicca saved her life and helped her strengthen herself to secure her release from an abusive marriage.

Moonwater has been practicing Wicca since 1990, first as a solitary and then in a coven.

Moonwater posts at her blog,

TheHiddenChildrenoftheGoddess.com.

(also known as **GoddessHasYourBack.com**)

She felt called to write the blog even through she is dyslexic. She works with a team of editors. She says, "I wish to educate those who don't understand what the Craft is about. Some people may not yet identify themselves as pagan, but they'd like more information."

Moonwater's blog now serves visitors from over 138 countries.

She has addressed college students in Comparative Religion classes for over ten years. She leads workshops. She lives with her cat Magick and her sweetheart of many years; he is one of her editors. She enjoys knitting and photography.

Her work is endorsed by Wiccan notables including Patrick McCollum (receiver of the Mahatma Gandhi Award for the Advancement of Pluralism).

Moonwater SilverClaw can be contacted at:

AskAWitchNow@gmail.com

Or at her blog:

TheHiddenChildrenoftheGoddess.com

(also known as GoddessHasYourBack.com)

Appendix
(including Cast Circle;
Cakes and Wine; Close Circle; Cleanse and
Consecrate an Object)

Cast Circle

Cast the Sacred Circle

Knock three times on the altar. Ring the bell three times.

Light the working candle with the lighter and set the candle down on the altar. (The other candles will be lit from it later using the taper.)

Light the charcoal (if you are using it) from the working candle. (The incense will placed on the charcoal later.)

Take your athame and place its tip into the flame of the working candle. Say:

I exorcise* you, o creature of fire. And I purify and bless you in the names of the Goddess and the God that you are pure and clean.

(*Note: When we speak of *exorcise* here, we are purifying the item by driving out any negative energies.)

Trace a pentacle (a five-pointed star) over the flame. Pick up the candle and raise it up above you and imagine the Gods' energy filling the flame. Place the candle back on the altar.

Take your athame and place its tip into the bowl of water. Say:

I exorcise you, o creature of water. And I purify and bless you in the names of the Goddess and the God that you are pure and clean.

Trace a pentacle in the water. Pick up the bowl of water

and raise it up above you and imagine the Gods' energy filling the water. Place the bowl back on the altar.

Take your athame and place its tip into the salt. Say:

I exorcise you, o creature of earth. And I purify and bless you in the names of the Goddess and the God that you are pure and clean.

Trace a pentacle in the salt. Pick up the bowl of salt and raise it up above you and imagine the Gods' energy filling the salt. Place the salt bowl back on the altar.

Take your athame and place its tip into the incense. Say:

I exorcise you, o creature of air. And I purify and bless you in the names of the Goddess and the God that you are pure and clean.

Trace a pentacle over incense. Pick up the incense and raise it up above you and imagine the Gods' energy filling the incense. Place the incense on the lit charcoal.

Take your athame and scoop up three blades of the salt. You may also use your finger. Put the three pinches of salt into the water and mix it with the blade of your athame to make consecrated water. Pick up the bowl of consecrated water and raise it up above you and imagine the Gods' energy filling it.

Take the consecrated water (the salt and water mixture) and dip your fingers into it. Dab some of it on your inner wrists and forehead. Say:

I bless myself with Earth and Water.

Take the censer filled with the burning incense and wave the smoke over you. Say:

I bless myself with Air and Fire.

Take the consecrated water and use your fingers to asperge (sprinkle with consecrated water) the circle boundary. Starting with the north and moving clockwise, walk a complete circle around the perimeter, paying especial attention to aspersing each corner as you go. When finished, place the bowl back on the altar.

Pick up the censer filled with the burning incense. Use your hand to wave the incense smoke around the circle. Starting with north and moving clockwise, walk a complete circle around the perimeter, waving the smoke as you go. Be careful not to burn yourself or anything else. When finished, place the censer back on the altar.

You have just cleansed the space and yourself. Now let's continue by casting the circle.

Take the athame. Envision energy being channeled from you and coming out the tip of your athame [You point the athame outward, away from you as you create the circle.] Starting with north and moving clockwise, walk a complete circle around the perimeter. As you walk, say:

I conjure you, o circle of power, that you be a boundary between the seen mundane world and the spirit world, that you protect me and contain the magick that I shall raise within you! I purify and bless you in the names of the Goddess and the God. So mote it be!

Finish at the east quarter (direction).

Now it's time to "call the quarters." (This refers to the four directions.)

Pick up the athame and the taper from the altar. Light the taper from the working candle. Go and stand in the east corner of where your circle boundary is. Starting with the east candle, say:

I call you up, o mighty ones of the East, element of Air. Come guard my circle and witness my rite.

Trace a pentacle in the air with your athame. Then taking the taper, light the quarter candle for east. Say:

Hail and welcome!

Move clockwise to the south candle. Say:

I call you up, o mighty ones of the South, element of Fire. Come guard my circle and witness my rite.

Trace a pentacle in the air with your athame. Then light the quarter candle for south. Say:

Hail and welcome!

Move clockwise to the west candle. Say:

I call you up, o mighty ones of the West, element of Water. Come guard my circle and witness my rite.

Trace a pentacle in the air with your athame. Then light the quarter candle for west. Say:

Hail and welcome!

Move clockwise to the north candle. Say:

I call you up, o mighty ones of the North, element of Earth. Come guard my circle and witness my rite.

Trace a pentacle in the air with your athame. Then light the quarter candle for north. Say:

Hail and welcome!

Return to the altar. Using the taper, light the Goddess candle, saying:

Welcome, my Lady!

Using the taper, light the God candle, saying:

Welcome, my Lord!

You have now completed casting your circle.

[Place ritual here.]

Cakes and Wine Ceremony

After any ritual, it is important to replenish and ground your energy. Begin with the wine or juice. Why? When you do ritual you are using up energy to create your magick working. You need to feed your body to replace these used energies. In this way you will stay strong and healthy.

Begin with the wine or juice. Take the cup from your altar and pour the wine or juice into it. Then take the athame and dip its tip into the wine or juice. Say:

As the athame is to the male, so the cup is to the female, and so joined bring union and harmony.

Pour some of your blessed wine or juice into the offering bowl or plate on your altar. Say:

To the Gods!

You can now partake of the beverage.

Take your athame and point it over the cake. Say:

Blessed be these cakes that they bestow health, peace, joy, strength, and that fulfillment of love that is perpetual happiness.

Take one of the cakes (or just a piece) and place it in the offering bowl or plate. Say:

To the Gods!

You can now partake of the blessed cakes.

So, what do you do with the blessed offerings in the offering dishes? You certainly don't just throw them into the garbage! They are gifts to the Gods. After you close circle take them outside to your garden where you can leave it on the ground to help nourish the Earth.

If you do not have a garden at your home, you can take the offerings out into the woods and leave them there. Some Wiccans who live in the city set the blessed offering out on their porch for local animals to partake. Be sure to only leave biodegradable food. Avoid wrappers or containers that will not decompose.

Closing Circle

It is very important to dismiss the energies you have called for your circle. Be sure to take down the magick temple (circle) you erected. And certainly dismiss the quarters!

<u>To close your circle:</u>

Take your athame and hold it up and stand facing the east. Say:

Hail East, the element of Air. I thank you for guarding my circle and witnessing my rite. May you depart to your fair and lovely realms. I bid you hail and farewell!

Trace a pentacle in the air with your athame.

Continuing, moving in a clockwise circle, stand facing the south. Say:

Hail South, the element of Fire. I thank you for guarding my circle and witnessing my rite. May you depart to your fair and lovely realms. I bid you hail and farewell!

Trace a pentacle in the air with your athame.

Moving clockwise around the circle, stand facing the west. Say:

Hail West, the element of Water. I thank you for guarding my circle and witnessing my rite. May you depart to your fair and lovely realms. I bid you hail and farewell!

Trace a pentacle in the air with your athame.

Moving clockwise around the circle, stand facing the north. Say:

Hail North, the element of Earth. I thank you for guarding my circle and witnessing my rite. May you depart to your fair and lovely realms. I bid you hail and farewell!

Trace a pentacle in the air with your athame.

Return again to the north, walking clockwise, walk the boundary of the circle, and say:

Fire seal the circle round,

Let it fade beneath the ground,

Let all things be as they once were before.

The circle is now no more,

Merry meet, merry part,
And merry meet again!
So mote it be!

* * * * * *

How to Cleanse, Bless and Consecrate An Object

Take the object you wish to be cleansed and consecrated.

Step 1) Dip your fingers in your holy water, lightly dab the object and say:
I cleans you with Earth and Water.

Step 2) Pass the object through the incense smoke and say:
I Bless and Consecrate you with Air and Fire.

You have now cleansed and consecrated your object.

Excerpt from *The Hidden Children of the Goddess* by Moonwater SilverClaw

THE HIDDEN CHILDREN OF THE GODDESS:
EMBRACE WICCA, BECOME STRONG, BE AT PEACE WITH YOURSELF AND THE WORLD AROUND YOU

CHAPTER 13:
MAGICK, A HOW-TO GUIDE

In this chapter we will explore what magick is and different ways to practice it. Let's start with a quote from Heinrich Cornelius Agrippa (1486-1535), who wrote books on occult philosophy:

> "Unless a man be born a magician, and God have destined him even from his birth to the work, so that spirits do willingly come of their own accord - which doth happen to few - a man must use only of those things herein set down, or written in our other books of occult philosophy, as means to fix the mind upon the work to be done; for it is in the power of the mind itself that spirits do come and go, and magical works are done, and all things in nature are but as uses to induce the will to rest upon the point desired."

From the above quote, we realize that most of us need to

study (including "books of occult philosophy") and practice. Only some are gifted "from his/her birth to the work." We must be diligent in our study and practice of magick. What exactly is magick? Magick (with a "k") is the practice of using the natural energies, the Earth, and heavenly bodies to create change in oneself and the environment.

As we do magick, we guide the natural energies around us. These natural energies are within us, around us, everywhere and at all times, from an old-growth forest to your office cubicle in the big city. What are these energies? They are the energies of the elements and the universe. As you learned in Chapter 6, the building blocks for all things are the Five Elements: Air, Fire, Water, Earth, and Spirit. Life can't survive without each of these. Because of this, everything exudes energy, including trees, the sun, rocks, and ourselves.

We use the Five Elements' energies and the other energies to help us create change in our lives. During rituals, we can also ask the Gods for help by lending us their energy. But for now let's talk about the energies around us.

Energy & Magick

Note of caution: When doing magick, always use the energies around you. Never use your personal energy. The idea is to pull in other energy instead of just relying on your own energy.

During rituals we raise energy, channel it through our bodies, and direct it through our will. Chapters 9 and 11 give instructions on how to achieve these goals. They explain how to raise and work with the energy around you, and how to channel the energy through your body. Chapter 9 provides meditation exercises in which you draw up energy from the earth, and Chapter 11 explains how to raise the energy needed to do magick. Raising energy is like charging a battery.

Your body is like a battery, like a conductor for power or energy. As I mentioned, you never want to use your own personal energy when practicing magick. Doing so will run down your body or your battery.

Instead, you raise energy and use this energy to power your spells and work. You direct the energy to do its purpose by focusing and willing it. (Soon, in the paragraphs below, I'll explain the process of concentration.)

How Magick works

Without the necessary knowledge, spells fail. I've seen friends disappointed as their spells went wrong. We notice that many people buy a book of spells and cast away, not knowing the how and why. Spells will do a giant belly flop on you if this is what you do without the knowledge of how magick works in the first place.

Intent

To do successful magick, you need to understand several things. First, you must have an intent. You need to know what you want to manifest. I know this sounds simple, but many people just don't think the intent through.

Let's say you want a car. Okay, why do you want a car? Is it to take you to your job? Or is it something you want to have people envy? Hey I don't judge. But if you just say "I want a car" to the universe, you are likely to get that Pinto down the block.

Let's say you just moved to a new area and you need a car

to get you around. You want something nice but economical. You don't want a piece of junk that will break down on you every chance it gets. I suggest you go shopping, whether it be on the internet or at a car lot. Get to know what you want and like for your car.

When you pick out features, you're attaching specific desires to the car. This will help manifest the car you want versus the junk heap down the block. Refine your image of the perfect car in your mind. Include other requirements you have like good gas mileage and inexpensive repair costs. The more specific you are with your intent, the less there will be unexpected results like getting the lemon down the lane.

Having a solid intent is your first step before you do any magick. Once you have that cornerstone set you can continue with the second thing which is concentration. During your spell you will need lots of concentration and visualization.

Visualization

We'll continue with the process of manifesting a particular car. You can use a toy car as a visualization focus object. As you stare at the toy car, you also use your mind to imagine getting into a real car and driving it. You can even take a number of steps further. For instance, if you desire a convertible car, you imagine the wind blowing through your hair as you drive with the top down.

Concentration

This is the process of focusing and then refocusing your mind on your visualization task. In essence, you concentrate on the object and on the images in your mind that are specific for your desired manifestation. It is natural for the mind to wander at times. When it does, you just consciously redirect your mind to focus on the visualization object once again.

Meditation

Some Wiccans begin with meditation to clear the mind before using both concentration and visualization. Let's return to the Tree of Life Meditation we covered in Chapter 9. Remember that you combined a focus on your breath with envisioning energy blossoming from your head as branches and from your feet as roots. (For specifics, return to Chapter 9).

Once you have cleansed your energy via the Tree of Life Meditation, you will focus on a shape—that is, a mental image of a shape (perhaps, a triangle or sphere). Using your mind's eye, view the shape from every angle. Concentrate on this shape for an extended time.

Willpower

The Collins English Dictionary defines willpower as "the ability to control oneself and determine one's actions."

Kelly McGonigal, Ph.D., author of *The Willpower Instinct*, wrote: "Willpower is about harnessing the three powers of I will, I won't and I want to help you to achieve your goals (and stay out of trouble)."

When it comes to successfully performing magick, willpower, to me, means the driving force of desire for some form of change. So I focus on the power of "I will." This is an important distinction because many people think of willpower as only the ability to avoid temptation.

The compelling observation is that Wiccans, who become proficient at these three processes of visualization, concentration, and meditation, actually strengthen their will. How? Once you do the three processes, you actually enhance your belief, and you push through your doubt.

Realize, you need to *will* something into being. This includes confidence that what you are doing will work. If you don't have that, your spell just won't become a reality.

You need your will for your intent to be as strong as possible. This is why when we are desperate for something, we can usually manifest it. Using your will is deeply rooted in your desire. Lack of will just creates another belly flop.

I've now shared with you the five *must-haves* (intent, visualization, concentration, meditation and willpower) for doing magick that works.

Now, let's talk about some of the other tools we use to manifest our desires.

When you start to create a spell, you begin with the intent. Once you have that strongly in place, you start crafting the wording of the spell. Be specific, and in this way you will avoid loopholes or misunderstandings in your magick. Vague wording leads to mistakes and disappointment. Remember, if you merely ask for a car, you might get one that is a piece of junk.

Another tool for working magick is using herbs that attract a particular thing or effect. For example, to attract money, Wiccans often use cinnamon. They also use sage for purifying spaces, people, and more.

I would suggest keeping things simple, at least to start with. Simple spells can be the most potent because they are easy to do.

An example of a simple technique is to appease the Younger Self, which can be considered one's inner child. The Feri (Fairy) tradition calls this part of ourselves "Sticky Self." The Younger Self (inner child) likes to play. Younger Self likes song, dance, rhyme, and all the sparkly shiny things in life. She/he likes rattles and other objects which we can use as tools to connect with Younger Self.

Why am I talking about Younger Self? Wiccans use Younger Self as a messenger to the Gods. You need to keep Younger Self's attention so that she/he gets the message right. This may sound silly, but doing things that would keep a five-year-old happy in your magick is a good start. This is one reason why we use feathers, incense, candles, and other tools in our magick. There are other reasons, too. Everything has its own energy and meaning. Such energy and meaning help you focus and add power to the work that you do. Don't forget this is work. It takes a lot of energy and concentration to do spell work and magick in general.

So you have your intent and your words in rhyme. You have added other elements to make Younger Self happy and to lend extra meaning/power to your magick. At this point, once you have gathered all that you need, you cast circle. Do the spell by using your items to focus on your intent. Chant your words and use a power-raising technique (all while keeping keen concentration on your intent).

The next step is important. Without this step, you might as well not have done all the previous efforts. What step am I talking about? You need to let all that energy you raised and all that focus go. That's right, you need to release it into the universe so that it can do the job you set it out to do. This lets Younger Self carry your message to the Gods and to create the change you desire.

We will continue to talk about spells and their wording below.

The Tools of Magick

We don't really need anything but our own bodies to do magick, although most Wiccans use props/tools/elements such as candles and incense to help with the process. Many of us need these tools to help us channel (focus) our raised energy or power toward the task we need to accomplish.

Doing magick is not all about the physical tools of the trade. If you read the old grimoires (textbooks about magick), you know that they talk about consecrated swords and pentacles and using hard-to-get incense and herbs. But the old masters knew that the most potent tool in your toolbox is your mind. Still, Younger Self really likes the material objects!

How do we awaken and use our minds? It's all about motivation and determination! It's about how emotionally connected and invested you are. You will receive the best results if you feel strongly about what you are working toward.

How invested are you? Remember we talked about intent, concentration, and will. Do you meditate and study on your desire, or do you go shopping instead? Do you buy a book on the subject, or do you go to a bar with your friends?

Take some time to clear your mind before you begin doing magick. I know this from experience. One time I did a ritual to increase prosperity, but my mind was still full of fear. Not only did the prosperity ritual fail to work, things went the other way! I actually lost some money to a mix-up at the bank!

So make sure to clear your mind and put yourself into a calm state of being. After you have done this, think about what you want to accomplish. Then concentrate your mind on your desire. Write it down to help clarify and solidify it. Focus on the essence of your work and narrow it down to a simple chant or phrase that you can concentrate on during your magick work.

The Clause

I find it very important to include the clause "an it harm none" (from *The Wiccan Rede*) at the end of the spoken spell. I also include it at the end of spells that are only written down and never used. There is a good reason for this: Words matter. It keeps the spell from harming you or anyone else. Also, it's just not possible to see the many ripples a spell might produce. Even the most carefully worded spell could have unforeseen effects, and may include an undesired negative result. Wording and intention are the keys to doing magick successfully.

Clarity of purpose is paramount. A spell that says, "I want more money in my life" is an open-ended statement. Try asking in a more specific way, like, "Let money find me in any way legal, with ease, love, and luck for me and everyone involved around me." Close your request with a clause like "an it harm none" or "for the good of all involved." This will guide your magick toward a successful outcome that will benevolent toward everyone involved.

End of Excerpt from *The Hidden Children of the Goddess* by Moonwater SilverClaw

* * * * * *

Excerpt from *Beyond the Law of Attraction to Real Magic*
by Moonwater SilverClaw

Beyond the Law of Attraction to Real Magick
How You Can Remove Blocks to Prosperity, Happiness and Inner Peace

Self-perspective: Overcome the Blockage of Not Feeling Worthy

Do you feel worthy of the best that life has to offer?
Maybe on the conscious level you say, "Sure. Bring it on. The
new house, new car, and a real, loving relationship."

But have you ever sabotaged your chances of getting
exactly what you wanted?

Self-sabotage can occur because of feeling not worthy on a
subconscious level.

If it's subconscious, how can we deal with this?

Good question.

Soon I will share with you a Self-Love meditation.

But first let's talk about magick. The whole premise of this
book is that there is a way to go about the Law of Attraction
with more power.

To put it simply, the Law of Attraction is a form of
magick, but people who read an introductory book on the
Law of Attraction are often denied enough information to
truly make the Law of Attraction work in their own lives.

So to really make a positive difference in your life, we
need to talk about real magick. I spell magick with a "k" to
distinguish it from stage magic you see on television.

Magick is a natural power, *not* a supernatural one. Who
uses magick? In my spiritual path, Wicca, one is trained to
use magick in appropriate ways.

When Wiccans do magick, they channel *natural* energies and create change with them.

Well, if Wicca isn't really supernatural, then why practice Wicca at all?

To put it simply, *you want something.* That's probably why you were interested in the Law of Attraction in the first place. Now in the context of learning real magick, you'll be able to fully use the Law of Attraction. And that's good news!

Everyone is different and has their own answer to that question. I like to think of religion as a bottle of wine. Let's say you have three different people who all taste the same bottle of wine. The first person points out that the flavor has accents of oak. The second praises the hints of apple in it, and the third enjoys the floral notes. They are all right. The wine contains all the flavors they described. But each person detected something different. Religion is like that. Deity can't be entirely known. So the truth of it is scattered into many faiths.

In Wicca, we honor the God and the Goddess. If that's new to you, you can substitute the label of Higher Power or God or Deity.

The Gods and Goddesses have helped me and they can help you, too. The first thing they taught me was self-love.

Before we go further, let's make a distinction between self-love and self-conceit (or being stuck in one's ego).

Self-love is about kindness and support. So it's a good thing. It is NOT about your ego or puffing yourself up.

Let me show you how the Gods changed my perspective on myself for the better.

One of the best exercises I learned is meditation. Through reflective meditation, the Gods helped me understand how skewed my perception of myself really was. This was a key turning point for me.

One thing you always hear about are affirmations, but for many of us these just don't work.

First, let's cover what an affirmation is. It's a personal, positive statement. It can be as simple as "I feel terrific" or "I make a lot of money."

For many, the above statements don't work. Why?

A number of people have said, "It just sounds like I'm lying to myself."

Like myself, many people's inner self-beliefs interfere with these positive statements. For an example, if I used the affirmation "I am thin," my brain would object with "No, I'm not. Look in the mirror." It's not true. No matter how hard you try to pound that new idea into your brain, your brain pounds just as hard back.

So how did the Gods help me deal with this problem? They inspired me to create a Self-Love Meditation.

So instead of the uphill battle of an affirmation, we'll use the Self-Love Meditation to work with the situation.

[End of above Excerpt from Beyond the Law of Attraction to Real Magick]

Purchase your copy of the above books (paperback or ebook) at
Amazon.com or BarnesandNoble.com
See **Free Chapters** of Moonwater SilverClaw's 3 books at http://amzn.to/1tni9WP

Special Offer Just for Readers of this Book:

Contact Moonwater SilverClaw at askawitchnow@gmail.com for special discounts on books, audio programs, video programs, consultations, workshops and presentations. Just mention your experience with this book. Thank you.

Made in the USA
Lexington, KY
20 February 2015